100 Ideas for Teaching

Knowledge and Understanding of the World

Alan Thwaites

continuum

Continuum International Publishing Group

The Tower Building	80 Maiden Lane
11 York Road	Suite 704
London	New York
SE1 7NX	NY 10038

www.continuumbooks.com

British Library Cataloguing-in-Publication Data
A catalogue record for this book is available from the British Library.

ISBN: 978-0-8264-9868-7 (paperback)

Designed and typeset by Kenneth Burnley, Wirral, Cheshire
Printed and bound in Great Britain by MPG Books Ltd, Bodmin, Cornwall

Contents

Acknowledgements   ix

Introduction   xi

Section 1: Birth–11 months

1	Keep Smiling	2
2	Name that Nose	3
3	Baby Rock and Roll	4
4	Now You See It, Now You Don't	6
5	Roll a Ball	7
6	Sound Bites	8
7	Ooh, Aah, Ouch!	9
8	Diddle Diddle Dumpling	11
9	Incy Wincy Spider	12
10	Get the Picture	13
11	Doorbells	14
12	Pots and Pans	15

Section 2: 8–20 months

13	Bowling Alley	18
14	Ten Little Fingers	19
15	Round and Round the Garden	20
16	Build it Up	21
17	Ups and Downs	22
18	Slowly, Slowly Goes the Snail	24
19	The Three Little Pigs	25
20	What's Cooking?	26
21	The Wheels on the Bus	28
22	What Weather!	29
23	Cars, Trains and Planes	31
24	Who's Calling Please?	33
25	Weather Watch	34
26	Walkies!	36
27	Strictly Dancing	37

Section 3: 16–26 months

28	Hot and Cold	40
29	Doctor, Doctor	41
30	Old MacDonald	42
31	Phone Errands	43
32	Keep Moving	44
33	Dolly's Day	45
34	Memory Cushions	46
35	Copy It	47
36	Cue 'Pat-a-Cake'	48
37	Skittles	49
38	Feed the Birds	50
39	Press the Button	52
40	Water Wonders	53
41	Super Sand	54

Section 4: 22–36 months

42	Car Run	56
43	Welcome!	57
44	Snap Happy	58
45	What a Day!	59
46	Match the Room	60
47	Puzzle Animals	61
48	Puzzle People	62
49	Odd One Out	63
50	Postie!	64
51	All Day, All Night	65
52	Town Mouse	66
53	Country Mouse	67
54	Kim's Game	68
55	Monday Fun-day	69
56	Garden Safari	70
57	Find the Fruit	71
58	This is the Way	72
59	Row the Boat	73

Section 5: 30–50 months

60	Sorted!	76
61	Build it with Bricks	77
62	Make Music	78
63	Mousey, Mousey	79

64	Building Site	80
65	Bridge It	81
66	Gone Fishing	82
67	Bread	83
68	Noah's Ark	85
69	Butterflies	86
70	All Dressed Up	87
71	The Enormous Turnip	88
72	Leaf Prints	90
73	Right up your Street	91
74	Bobo's House	92
75	Baby Animals	93
76	Nesting	94
77	Bobo's Birthday	95
78	Mouldy Bread and Cheese!	96
79	Winging It	97
80	Circle Animals	98
81	Face Up to It	99
82	Turning Over a New Leaf	100
83	What's My Line?	101

Section 6: 40–60+ months

84	Balloons: Up and Away	104
85	Balloons: Static Electricity	106
86	Chasing Shadows	107
87	Me and My Shadow	108
88	What Do You Feel?	109
89	What's That Smell?	110
90	Flower Power	111
91	Sow the Seeds	112
92	Recording!	114
93	What's That?	115
94	Clues from the Past	117
95	Disability Awareness	118
96	Calling Planet Earth	119
97	It's a Sign	120
98	Recycle It	122
99	It is My Belief	123
100	Who Lives Here?	125

Acknowledgements

Judith Thwaites has provided many of the ideas presented in this book, together with support and encouragement, for which I am very grateful. Special thanks to Penny Tassoni.

Introduction

Children acquire many sophisticated skills and abilities before starting full-time education, making their pre-school experiences vital for their future education. The ground rules for life are laid in the first years. Provision for the care of those aged 0–5 years can vary depending on parental circumstances and wishes, and there are similar variations in the type of care available outside the home. A child beginning primary education who has received good quality care and learning experiences, whether that be entirely at home or with a combination of various early years providers, will be confident and eager to learn.

Even before birth, babies are sensing the world around them. From the moment they enter the world and the exploration and investigation really begins, they thrill at discovering everything for the first time. Their growing awareness and abilities serve only to spur them on to learn and understand more. This book offers discovery activities for pre-school care providers wishing to capitalize on the enthusiasm of the children and their desire to learn.

Using this book

If you enjoy using this book then so will the children in your care. The activities have been chosen for their enjoyment and play value. The need for elaborate or expensive resources has been kept to a minimum. Ideas for extension or innovation are included where appropriate. Childcare providers are obviously very aware of health and safety issues, but it is hoped that none will be offended if a health and safety note is included with many of the activities. The intention has been, first of all, to provide a user-friendly set of ideas with a real value to the children.

There is no recommended, or even suggested, duration for any of the activities. Clearly, this will depend on the age, stage of development and, above all, the interest of the children. Some ideas stand alone but many are designed to be worked in with the regular sessions and routines of the day. It is assumed also that any activity, once started, would be modified or changed altogether should the enjoyment level be lost. It is very likely that any given activity will work one day but not another or will work for one child but not another. It is expected you will enjoy adapting and innovating and will put your own personal stamp on the interaction with the children in your care.

Statutory Framework for the Early Years Foundation Stage

Provision for pre-school children in its widest sense has, for the first time, been brought together by the Government within its Statutory Framework for the Early Years Foundation Stage (EYFS) 2007 (obtainable as a download from www.standards.dfes.gov.uk and www.publications.teachernet.gov.uk). The expectation is that the body of skills, abilities and knowledge outlined in the Framework will be developed through essentially enjoyable play activities and experiences within daily routines. Very young children, especially, need to learn and discover through enjoyment and play at their own pace.

It is not the purpose of this book to go into great detail about the EYFS Framework, briefly described below. It is assumed that all early years care providers will have had access to it and familiarized themselves with the requirements. However, the activities suggested in these pages are designed to assist with meeting the requirements of the EYFS and can be directly linked to the aspects and age groups set out in it.

The sections are arranged in the broad age groups of the EYFS. These age groups overlap somewhat, allowing for obvious variations in development. It is expected that the groupings will be used merely as a rough guide.

Most of the activities included for younger children can be used throughout all the age ranges, either as they stand or with minor modification. Thus, it will be possible to use almost all of the activities with children who are aged 4–5 years. Young children love to play favourite games and sing favourite songs over and over again. It builds confidence, as well as knowledge and skills.

With each of the 100 activities there is a reference to the relevant EYFS Knowledge and Understanding of the World aspect or, in many cases, more than one aspect.

The Knowledge and Understanding of the World Programme (EYFS)

Learning and Development, according to the Framework, covers six areas or programmes:

- Personal, Social and Emotional Development
- Communication, Language and Literacy
- Problem Solving, Reasoning and Numeracy
- Knowledge and Understanding of the World
- Physical Development
- Creative Development.

Each of these areas is further divided into aspects of learning, the number of these varying between programmes. This book is concerned with the

Knowledge and Understanding of the World programme but there will inevitably be overlaps with other programmes.

Knowledge and Understanding of the World

Aspect of learning	. . . is about
Exploration and Investigation	Using all senses to learn about the world around us. Using appropriate tools and methods to discover more. Finding similarities, differences and patterns in the natural and constructed environments. Discovering how things work and why they are used.
Designing and Making	Using a wide range of materials and objects to build and construct. Using the right tools and methods safely. Evaluating and adapting work.
Information and Communication Technology	Finding out about – and using where appropriate – the many forms of ICT and programmable toys.
Time	Developing a sense of past, present and future.
Place	Developing a sense of the natural and constructed features which identify the local environment.
Communities	Finding out about the people in the community, their relationships, occupations, cultures and beliefs.

The Knowledge and Understanding of the World area includes a growing awareness of regular festivals, such as Christmas and Diwali. There are no specific activities for these here as it is assumed they will be given suitable emphasis at the time. Also, it is assumed that children will have regular access to a number of sophisticated toys which are operated with buttons and switches for the ICT aspect of this area of learning. Good quality items of this nature are vital for enhancing children's understanding of their world.

Remember also that there is no substitute for a wide selection of good quality books – both fiction and non-fiction – for sharing with the children.

In addition to the resources mentioned in each idea the following might also be useful:

- Toy keyboards and other instruments.
- Battery-operated toys.
- Toys which make a noise on the pull of a lever or the press of a button.
- Constructional toys.
- Stories, traditional rhymes and games from ethnic communities.
- Visits from people of different cultural backgrounds or with particular skills.

This book, however, sets out to provide low-cost activities which use you as the main resource.

Section 1:
Birth–11 months

Children of this age soak up all the messages and signals that all their senses experience. Full understanding of what they hear, see, touch, smell and taste will come through the security of constant contact, repetition and enjoyment. Most of these first activities should be developed into the older age groups as independence grows. For babies not yet walking, experiences need to be brought to them. Constant talk about sights, sounds, smells, taste and what things feel like to the touch is vital to the development of understanding, even though the child cannot vocalize fully.

Keep Smiling

EYFS aspect	Group size	Resources
Exploration and Investigation Communities	Individual	None

Focus on the way babies concentrate intensely on people's faces and enjoy one-to-one interaction. Their means of expression at this young age consists of smiling or chuckling, gurgling, wriggling and waving limbs about.

- With the baby clean and comfortable, spend a minute or two getting to know one another.
- Pay the baby compliments in a confident, grown-up voice, 'Oh, you're gorgeous!' 'Aah, I love your little button nose.' Engage the baby, look happy and make lots of eye contact. Enjoy the 'conversation' and when the baby smiles, gurgles or waves arms and legs about, respond to her/his communication clearly with more of your own positive talking and body language. Use the baby's name throughout.
- Clap your hands, gently grasp the baby's hands and softly clap them together, saying, 'Clap, clap, clap.'
- Hold the baby's feet and move the legs gently to the rhythm of a short rhyme or song.
- Play 'peep-bo' by making your hands into shutters over your face (use your thumbs at your temples to act as 'hinges' to open and close the shutters).
- Repeat with your hands near – but not on – the baby's face and enjoy the fun together.

Name that Nose

EYFS aspect	Group size	Resources
Exploration and Investigation Time	Individual	None

When the baby is nappy-changed, clean and comfortable, use the quality time to introduce naming of facial features in a relaxed way.

Build up baby's attention with gentle communications, for example smiling, wiggling your fingers, stroking the baby's cheek, saying her/his name gently.

- Point to your own nose, saying 'nose' and smiling at the baby. Now gently press the baby's nose and repeat 'nose' in the same tone of voice.
- Repeat briefly with chin, eyes, mouth, ears and cheeks; gently draw your fingers over both the baby's eyebrows at the same time (very soothing). Always name your own facial features first, then the baby's.

If this is repeated fairly frequently over a period of time, the baby will learn to anticipate the naming words with the pressing or stroking of their counterpart facial features and will wriggle and kick with pleasure.

Taking this further

Name toes, tummy, fingers, knees (just the baby's – no need to tie yourself in knots for this). When the baby starts to talk she/he will already have this group of words stored away as part of her/his rich vocabulary.

IDEA
3
Baby Rock and Roll

EYFS aspect	Group size	Resources
Exploration and Investigation Place	Individual	A favourite toy or blanket or musical toy that attracts the baby's attention

Focus on the baby's ability to roll over and help her/him to actively explore the surroundings. At some point around five months, babies may surprise their carer by suddenly being able to roll over, when the day before they could not.

- When the baby is clean, comfortable and receptive, lay her/him on her/his back. Let the baby cuddle the blanket or toy or wind up a musical toy to focus interest.
- Gently take the blanket or toy away and talk to the baby while you let her/him see you placing the object about a metre away – just out of reach.
- Try to maintain the baby's attention on the object and if she/he wants to reach it you may, if necessary, very gently 'nudge' the baby to perform a roll towards the object. Do not intervene in the actual roll as the baby will have perfected her/his own safe way of rolling.
- Letting the baby hold and enjoy the object, pick the baby up and praise her/him.
- If the baby knows you well she/he may roll towards you instead of an object – this is more likely if there is nothing more interesting in the opposite direction.
- Rolling is obviously easier for the baby without a nappy on, if you are happy to chance it.

Safety note
Once a baby reaches the stage of being nearly or fully able to roll over, carers generally stop doing nappy changes on a raised surface, so the floor is a safer place for this activity.

Taking this further

When the baby starts to crawl or 'bum shuffle' and, later on, when she/he is taking early steps, you can use the above strategy to encourage efforts. If you are a key person, the baby will happily crawl/walk towards you for a cheer and a cuddle.

Now You See It, Now You Don't

EYFS aspect	Group size	Resources
Exploration and Investigation	Individual	A range of small, baby-safe animal toys

This is the classic now-you-see-it, now-you-don't game. Very young children can be propped up with cushions, put in a baby bouncer or held on a lap.

- Stimulate the child's interest with a few toy animals, talking about them and making sound effects.
- Choose one of the toys to start.
- When the child's eyes are watching the animal, make it suddenly disappear with, 'Oh, where's (the cat) gone?'
- Make (the cat) reappear.
- Play with (the cat) before repeating the game with another toy animal.

Taking this further
Older children might enjoy it if you swap the animal behind the cushion so that a different toy appears instead of the original.

Roll a Ball

EYFS aspect	Group size	Resources
Exploration and Investigation	Individual	Several soft balls of different colours (small enough for the baby to grasp but big enough to avoid swallowing) Large plastic dinner plate Shallow cardboard box

For this activity, young children unable to sit confidently should be cradled in a lap or put in a bouncy chair. You will need to use both hands some of the time.

- Introduce a soft, squashy ball (preferably not fluffy as this can prevent easy rolling). Talk about the feel and colour.
- When the child has handled it, place it on the plate and let it roll around gently.
- Make a game of stopping it to pick it up. Who can catch it easily?
- Try it with different coloured balls, pointing out the differences and comparing them with similar colours in the room.
- Allow the ball to roll off the edge of the plate (somewhere easy to retrieve) and make a game of finding it.
- Put the ball into a shallow cardboard box or box lid, easy to reach into but with sides to prevent the ball rolling out. Try the game again. This time the movement will be more random as the ball bounces off the sides of the box.
- Finish with offering three or four different coloured balls for the child to choose her/his favourite to play with on her/his own while you watch.

 Taking this further
You could ask the child to select a particular colour ball.

IDEA

6

Sound Bites

EYFS aspect	Group size	Resources
Exploration and Investigation	Individual	Light plastic or wooden beater Objects to hit – wooden, plastic, metallic, padded or soft

This is to show the different sounds made from hitting different objects or surfaces. With very young children, you will need to do all of the banging. Older children will naturally produce sounds in this way, of course, but this activity will direct their senses a little more.

- Introduce the beater, ensuring that the child is safe to use it.
- Help the child with hitting different objects in turn, pointing out sound differences.
- Notice the difference between a suspended piece of wood, plastic or metal and the same piece left flat on a surface.

Taking this further

Make a tune with the various 'notes'.

Ooh, Aah, Ouch!

EYFS aspect	Group size	Resources
Exploration and Investigation Designing and Making	1–2	Small shoebox or similar 'bed' for small soft toy or doll Three differently textured fabrics large enough to cover the soft toy/doll – two soft and cuddly, e.g. fleece fabric, flannelette; one rough or stiff, e.g. card, hessian

This activity uses touch to distinguish between textures.

- Lay a folded flannel or similar to represent a mattress in the bottom of a box.
- Tell the children it's time to put teddy (or whatever) to bed.
- Ask the child for help to wash his face, clean his teeth and kiss him goodnight.
- Lay teddy in the box.
- Say, 'Brrrr, it's cold. Let's make teddy warm, shall we?'
- Hold up each rectangle of fabric in turn to your own cheek, smiling and saying, 'Aaah' or 'Ooh' for the soft ones and 'Ouch' with a frown for the rough one. Each time, also hold it to the baby's face or to her/his hand and repeat the noises.
- You could slowly shake your head and say, 'No, that's not nice and soft for teddy, let's have this one. It's nice and soft, isn't it?'

Safety note
Plastic materials are not safe in case the children cover their faces or mouths.

 Taking this further
Ask children to pass the soft blanket for teddy or to put the hard blanket on the chair.

Let children handle and cuddle the fabrics in their own time. Encourage them to say 'Aaah' for soft and 'Ouch' for rough.

Diddle Diddle Dumpling

EYFS aspect	Group size	Resources
Exploration and Investigation Time	Individual	Child's own shoes

Enjoy the old nursery rhyme. This one is good to use during nappy changing, once the messy part is over. With the child comfortably on her/his back, sing or chant the rhyme, with actions:

Diddle diddle dumpling, my son John (take hold of the feet and wiggle the legs to the rhythm)
Went to bed with his trousers on,
One shoe off (take off a shoe or bootee or tickle the foot)
And one shoe on, (put on a shoe or bootee or tickle the other foot)
Diddle diddle dumpling, my son John.

Taking this further

You can vary the words to suit the occasion or to extend the awareness of clothing items. For example:

Diddle diddle dumpling, my son John
Went to (bed/town/park) with his (raincoat/woolly hat/t-shirt) on,
One (glove/sock/boot) off and one (glove/sock/ boot) on,
Diddle diddle dumpling, my son John.

Incy Wincy Spider

EYFS aspect	Group size	Resources
Exploration and Investigation	Individual	None

This is an ideal rhyme for introducing creepy crawlies as well as the weather.

With the child comfortably sitting or on her/his back, sing or chant the rhyme, with actions:

> *Incy Wincy spider, climbed up the spout* (walk fingers up the tummy)
> *Down came the rain* (wiggle fingers in the air) *and washed the spider out* (indicate with hands)
> *Out came the sunshine* (spread arms and hands in the air) *and dried up all the rain*
> *Incy Wincy spider climbed up the spout again.* (walk fingers up the tummy)

Taking this further

With older children, try including this with a book-sharing session on insects and spiders.

Get the Picture

EYFS aspect	Group size	Resources
Exploration and Investigation	Individual	Picture book

This is for those children who can sit confidently on a lap and enjoy sharing a good book.

Choose a book which includes large, colourful pictures of single items such as animals or things in the home. Talk about each picture to the child, making whatever sound effects and actions you can, for example:

- Train (sound)
- Telephone (sound and mime action)
- Lollipop (mime a licking action)
- Socks (mime pulling them on).

Taking this further

Older children will become more involved when they recognize the pictures, pointing at them and making their own noises and actions.

IDEA

11

Doorbells

EYFS aspect	Group size	Resources
Exploration and Investigation ICT Communities	Individual	A second adult or older child Battery-operated bell or buzzer Wendy house (optional)

This activity shows how ringing a doorbell can communicate to another person that you want to be let in.

- Set up a cardboard 'gate' across an open internal doorway and fix a battery-operated bell or buzzer to it. A Wendy house or similar play corner would be ideal.
- Introduce the idea of visiting someone at their house. It could include a doll or teddy in a toy pushchair if the child is using one to help in the early stages of walking.
- Prime another, older, child or an adult to wait on the other side of the 'door' until the doorbell rings.
- Take the child to visit and help her/him to press the doorbell and wait.
- Make the usual friendly greetings when the door is answered and go inside when invited for a drink of squash/cup of tea and a game.
- On another occasion reverse the roles.

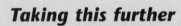

Taking this further

On any occasion when out and about and visiting, allow the child to press the doorbell and be involved with the resulting greetings. Involve the children, also, in receiving visitors if you are confident with the safety of the caller concerned. This would be even more beneficial if there is an entry phone system.

Pots and Pans

EYFS aspect	Group size	Resources
Exploration and Investigation	Individual	Wooden spoon or the plastic toy variety Plastic pots and pans

This activity can be started with very young babies, unable to sit up independently, but it can also be used at an increasingly advanced vocabulary level with older children up to two years.

- Choose a suitable item – in this example it is a wooden spoon but it could be any safe household object or a baby's toy.
- Ensure that the child is calm, peaceful and receptive.
- Talking gently to her/him, introduce the spoon, 'What's this? It's a spoon!'
- Encourage the child to take it and use all her/his senses to investigate it.
- At a suitable moment take the spoon and stir inside a toy plastic cooking pot (any empty, clean margarine or ice cream tub would be an alternative).
- Make plenty of rattling and banging noises with the spoon and pot, making sure the child is watching. Suggest that you are mixing up some dinner.
- Finish by miming eating from the spoon and let the child finish off the imaginary mixture.

Safety note
Ensure that there are no sharp edges to any object used. Do not share the spoon between mouths.

Taking this further

As the child becomes more aware and more mobile, she/he will take a more active role in these practical games, acting out household activities. A child who can confidently sit up, for example, will enjoy helping with the vacuuming using either a small toy cleaner or one home-made from kitchen roll tubes.

Section 2:
8–20 months

Any of the activities in the previous section could be used for this age group. It is around this age that children really begin to appreciate nursery rhymes. They are invaluable for presenting a whole range of early concepts and their importance can easily be overlooked. Early years teachers in primary schools regularly bemoan the fact that children arrive with very little knowledge of them. A number are included here.

IDEA

13

Bowling Alley

EYFS aspect	Group size	Resources
Exploration and Investigation	1 or 2	Several baby-safe balls of different sizes, weights, colours and surface textures Skittles or similar as a target

This game develops manipulation while giving experience of handling different materials.

- Begin by generally playing with one of the balls, passing it to and fro.
- Move on to setting up a target to roll the ball towards.
- Bring in each of the other balls in turn, describing them as they are included – 'Let's try the fluffy/squeezy/green/big/small/heavy ball.'
- Congratulate every attempt at hitting the target, remembering that the children are only aiming in the general direction at this stage.
- Finish with a decision on which was the 'best ball' for the game, even if there was not actually a best ball.

Safety note
Avoid throwing the balls at the target.

 Taking this further

Extend the 'alley' to make the target more difficult.

Involve the child in discussing the 'best ball for the job'.

Ten Little Fingers

EYFS aspect	Group size	Resources
Exploration and Investigation	Individual	None

This game extends the sensory aspects of the old favourite rhyme.

With the child on your lap or in a comfortable position, go through the rhyme with the actions:

> *I have ten little fingers and ten little toes,* (tweak the fingers and toes one at a time or all together)
> *Two little arms and one little nose,* (waggle the arms and tweak the nose)
> *One little mouth and two little ears,* (finger on lips and tweak the ears)
> *Two little eyes for smiles and tears,* (blink two or three times)
> *One little head and two little feet,* (nod the head and stamp the feet)
> *One little chin makes me all complete!* (tap the chin with a finger)

Round and Round the Garden

EYFS aspect	Group size	Resources
Exploration and Investigation	1–2	None

Use these sensory rhymes to focus on children's relationship with their environment.

Sitting quietly with the child next to you or on your lap, hold the child's hand, palm upwards, in your own palm. With the finger of your other hand, draw circles on the child's hand as you say:

> *Round and round the garden*
> *Like a teddy bear*
> *One step* (with the same finger, lightly touch the inside of the child's forearm)
> *Two steps* (touch the inside bend of the elbow)
> *Tickle you under there!* (very carefully tickle under the arm)

With this action rhyme, sit the child safely in front of you:

> *Knock on the door* (gently tap the child's forehead)
> *Lift the latch* (lift the hair)
> *Peep in* (look into the eyes)
> *Turn the key* (tweak the nose)
> *Walk in.* (gently walk your fingers on the child's lips)

With this one the child could sit opposite, mirroring your actions:

> *Two little eyes to look around* (point to your eyes)
> *Two little ears to hear each sound* (waggle your ears with your fingers)
> *One little nose to smell what's sweet* (touch and sniff)
> *One little mouth that likes to eat.* (touch your lips and make lip-smacking noises)

Build It Up

EYFS aspect	Group size	Resources
Exploration and Investigation	1–4	Set of building bricks

Young children will naturally place bricks on top of one other. They simply need guiding hands to see the potential. Here are some suggestions:

- Help the child to build a tower and carefully knock it down if it does not fall down sooner.
- Build a bridge so that toys can cross it or go under it.
- Build a house and make up little stories about the people who live there.
- Arrange the bricks into steps for a toy to climb onto a box or a low chair.
- Make a walled area for toy farm animals or parking places for cars.

Without necessarily expressing it in words, try to make any scene bring out the concept of building for a purpose. Naturally, from the child's point of view it is all play.

Taking this further
Children will progress naturally into increasing independence and making more sophisticated buildings.

IDEA 17

Ups and Downs

EYFS aspect	Group size	Resources
Exploration and Investigation	Individual	Props to help with telling the rhymes (optional)

These nursery rhymes are all associated with going up and down in some way. They are fun to do animatedly with the child. Pick just two or three favourites to do in any one session.

For this first one, march with the child up and down imaginary hills:

> *The Grand Old Duke of York*
> *He had ten thousand men.*
> *He marched them up to the top of the hill*
> *And he marched them down again.* (turn and go back)
> *And when they were up they were up* (stretch whole body and arms up)
> *And when they were down they were down* (stoop down and touch the floor)
> *And when they were only halfway up* (half straighten up)
> *They were neither up nor down.* (shake head and point up, then down)

If the child is Humpty Dumpty in this rhyme she/he can 'fall' from the lap, sideways onto a sofa or cushion, after a lot of wobbling.

> *Humpty Dumpty sat on the wall,*
> *Humpty Dumpty had a great fall.*
> *All the King's horses and all the King's men*
> *Couldn't put Humpty together again.*

Other rhymes to try:

- 'Jack and Jill'
- 'Hickory, Dickory, Dock'
- 'Hush-a-Bye Baby'
- 'Seesaw, Marjory Daw'

Safety note
Normal care should be taken when picking up children and moving their legs and arms.

Taking this further

Rhymes like, 'The Grand Old Duke of York' and 'Humpty Dumpty' could be acted out with larger groups of children who are a little older.

Slowly, Slowly Goes the Snail

EYFS aspect	Group size	Resources
Exploration and Investigation Place Communities	Individual	None

This is all about the movement of various creatures. It is best done with the child on your lap, which is definitely necessary for the horse-riding part.

Think of the animals you are going to use. Essentially, your fingers move up and down the arms and tummy of the child in the style of the creature. Appropriate soft toys can be used to add realism.

These are suggestions. No doubt you will think up some more:

- Slowly, slowly goes the snail . . . dragging along his sticky tail.
- See the hoppity rabbit hop . . . going so fast he cannot stop.
- Now see how the snake can glide . . . slithering slowly side to side.
- Chicken walks and stops for a peck . . . better watch he's not near your . . . neck!
- Elephant stomps in heavy strides . . . giving children wonky rides.
- Monkey swings from tree to tree . . . no one can . . . JUMP . . . as far as he!

Incorporate the old favourite, 'This is the Way the Lady Rides' with the child 'riding' on your knees, facing you and held securely by the hands.

This is the way the lady rides . . . amble, amble, amble (sway your legs gently to and fro)
This is the way the gentleman rides . . . trot, trot, trot (bounce your legs gently up and down)
This is the way the doctor rides . . . galloping, galloping, galloping. (bounce your legs up and down fast – remembering to hold on to the child)

Taking this further

The child can say the 'amble, amble, amble' bits at the end of each line. This can be great fun, especially while she/he is being galloped up and down (but be warned, it may lead to hiccups!).

IDEA

19

The Three Little Pigs

EYFS aspect	Group size	Resources
Exploration and Investigation Designing and Making	1–4	A copy of *The Three Little Pigs* (optional) Straw (shredded paper or hamster bedding) Sticks (cut strips of cardboard) Bricks (interlocking toy bricks) Toys to represent the three pigs and a wolf

Dramatize the story, using substitute materials to represent straw, sticks and bricks. You could start by reading the story or go straight into your own version, with the props. Encourage the children to help you do the house building with the various materials as they come into the story.

Tell the story with as much drama as possible, without being too scary when you come to the wolf's part.

Remember to emphasize the important parts:

- The strengths and weaknesses of the building materials – blow the 'straw' and 'sticks' away but show that you are unable to do the same with the bricks.
- The first and second pigs are lazy in using the straw and sticks.
- The third pig is a hard worker and is clever enough to trick the wolf.

IDEA 20

What's Cooking?

EYFS aspect	Group size	Resources
Exploration and Investigation Designing and Making	Individual	Props to help with telling the rhymes (optional)

These nursery rhymes are all loosely associated with food and cooking. Again, they are fun to do animatedly with the child. Pick just two or three favourites to do in any one session.

Pat the tummy and pretend to draw the letters on the child for this first one:

Pat-a-cake, pat-a-cake, baker's man
Bake me a cake as fast as you can
Pat it and prick it and mark it with 'B' (can be the initial letter of the child if it rhymes with 'me')
And put in the oven for baby (or child's name) *and me.*

This one provides a good excuse for a slow build up before suddenly running away:

Polly put the kettle on, Polly put the kettle on,
Polly put the kettle on, we all have tea.
Suki take it off again, Suki take it off again,
Suki take it off again, we all run away!

The names can be changed for the child's as familiarity with the original is established.

This one looks at hot food:

Pease porridge hot (blow)
Pease porridge cold (shiver)
Pease porridge in the pot
Nine days old. (yeugh! Pull a face)

Other rhymes to try:

* 'Jack Spratt'
* 'Old Mother Hubbard'

Safety note
Normal care should be taken when picking up children and moving their arms and legs.

Taking this further
Talk about hot and cold food and about refrigeration and why nine-day-old porridge is not good to eat.

IDEA 21

The Wheels on the Bus

EYFS aspect	Group size	Resources
Exploration and Investigation Communities	1–4	None

This is the old favourite that explores the characteristics of as many different types of people as you wish.

Talk about buses, bus drivers and where buses go. Sing the song 'The Wheels on the Bus' (with the children joining in if they are old enough).

The wheels on the bus go round and round, (make round movements with hands)
Round and round, round and round
The wheels on the bus go round and round,
All day long.

The next verses can be any person doing anything on the bus 'all day long'. Here are some suggestions:

- The driver on the bus says 'Sit tight, please'
- The dads on the bus go natter, natter, natter
- The grannies on the bus go 'Next stop, please'
- The babies on the bus go 'Wah!, Wah! Wah!'
- The uncles on the bus go nod, nod, nod
- The aunties on the bus go 'Hasn't he grown!'
- The granddad on the bus says 'This is my stop'.

Taking this further

Make your own bus with furniture and cushions and play a game of getting on and off the bus at local stops, for example at the library to choose a book, the dentist to have your teeth counted and the park to feed the ducks.

What Weather!

EYFS aspect	Group size	Resources
Exploration and Investigation	1–4	None

Enjoy some weather rhymes on a rough day, including actions wherever you can.

Rain, rain, go away
Come again another day.
Wind, wind, stop your whoosh
I don't like it when you push.
Sun, sun, keep shining down
Brighten up our lovely town.
Don't let the clouds hide your face
Send them away without a trace.
Snow, snow, snow some more
My boots are waiting at the door.

Dr Foster went to Gloucester
In a shower of rain
He stepped in a puddle right up to his middle
And never went there again.

I hear thunder, I hear thunder,
Hark, don't you? Hark, don't you?
Pitter patter raindrops.
Pitter patter raindrops.
I'm wet through, so are you.

Take advantage of any rough weather and go out and enjoy it as long as it is safe, if only for a few minutes.

Make up a story about what happened to a favourite toy when she/he went out in the wind and rain one day. In this example, the toy is Bobo the chimp.

Bobo the chimp loved windy days so he was very excited one day when he looked out and saw all the trees bending in the wind. He quickly put on his coat and his new red hat, picked up his umbrella and he set off to the park. The wind grew stronger . . . and stronger . . . and stronger until suddenly a gust of wind blew his hat right off his head. Bobo chased his hat down the path and across the grass. He was just about to catch it when, WHOOSH! The wind whisked it up into a tree where it stuck. Lucky I brought my umbrella, he thought, and he used it to hook his hat down. Just as he put his hat back on he felt a few drops of rain . . . and then some more . . . lots of rain. Bobo put up his umbrella but the wind was still strong. It was so strong, it blew his umbrella inside out. Bobo had a hard job hanging on to his umbrella and his hat at the same time. But the wind didn't care. It blew Bobo and his umbrella and his hat right through the park, right down the street and right back to his house. 'That was fun,' said Bobo, 'I hope it's windy again tomorrow!'

Taking this further

With older children, you could look at some of the after-effects of rough weather once it has calmed down.

Cars, Trains and Planes

EYFS aspect	Group size	Resources
Exploration and Investigation Place Time	1–4	None

Take the children on an imaginary journey, using as many forms of travel as possible and seeing as many things as you can dream of.

- Set up an imaginary vehicle, which could be a car or the seating area on a train, plane, bus, coach or boat.
- Think about where you are going – discuss it with the children if you are doing this with older ones.
- Explain the vehicle and decide who is sitting where at each stage of the journey, making sure they take a teddy, doll, blanket or suitable comforting toy.
- Show excitement, pointing out what you 'see' on the way and when you reach destinations.
- Start with getting up in the morning, having lunch somewhere in the middle and finish back at home or at a holiday destination, feeling tired and going to bed.

Taking this further

Journeys can be as simple or complicated as you like, but here is a suggestion for older children:

'Wake up! Wake up! Let's all get in the car. We're going off on holiday to Paris.'(Make sure the suitcases are in the boot and off you go to the ferry port.)

'The ferry at last! Look at all these cars and people waiting to get on. Let's go to the shops while we wait.'(Pile out and go to the shops for some imaginary items before returning to the car.)

'We're going on to the ferry now. I'm hungry. Let's buy some sandwiches to eat on the ferry.' (Change the car into a ferry lounge and enjoy the heaving of the waves as you wave goodbye to Dover and then hello to Calais.)

'Right! Here we are in France. Everybody back in the car. (Drive off towards Paris.)

'Here at last! Time for bed. We'll explore the city tomorrow.'

There can be any number of 'officials' on the journey, such as ticket-sellers, guides, customs officers, passport control – whatever is familiar to the children.

Who's Calling Please?

EYFS aspect	Group size	Resources
ICT	1–2	Toy phone

This game reinforces the idea that a telephone enables communication between two people.

Show the child the phone and clearly name it 'phone', 'telephone' or 'mobile'.

- Demonstrate pretend answering – pick up the phone, press the buttons if it is a mobile, hold it to your ear and say, 'Hello', 'Mm hmm', 'Yes, I see', etc. Then say, 'Bye', press the button and put it down.
- Position yourself slightly out of sight but keep in touch for the child's security.
- Make a ringing sound.
- Guide the child through the call, telling her/him when to pick up the phone and press the buttons.
- It is possible that towards the upper end of this age group the child will understand enough about phones to 'call' you, although it could all become a little confusing about whose turn it is to speak. It is much easier when the adult is guiding the conversation.

Safety note
Ensure that children know the difference between real and toy phones.

> ## Taking this further
> Give the child a task – ask her/him to phone 'Nana' to tell her we are coming on Tuesday or phone 'Daddy' to tell him he's got sausages for dinner tonight. Try to slip in a question that the child needs to answer, for example 'Daddy' asks, 'How many sausages can he have?' Encourage the child to tell 'Daddy' down the phone.

Weather Watch

EYFS aspect	Group size	Resources
Exploration and Investigation Time Place	1–2	An outdoor area, such as a yard, garden, park

This activity encourages awareness of various types of weather, extending vocabulary and use of the senses. It is important to remember the positives about bad weather – for example, we need rainwater, and snow can be fun.

Whenever the weather changes, grasp the opportunity to give the child experience of the different sights, sounds and sensations associated with the elements. Point out:

Sunshine
- Shadows.
- Colour of the sky and shapes of clouds (watch a cloud move across the sky).
- The need to shield the eyes and never look at the sun.

Wind
- Blowing leaves (can the children move the leaves gently just by blowing them?).
- Washing flapping.
- Wind sounds.
  Different kinds of wind – breeze, gale.

Rain
- Ripples made by raindrops in the puddles.
- The need to water the flowers and plants.
- Ponds filling up with water for the ducks and fish.
- The fun of wearing wellies and macs and splashing in puddles.
- Types of protective clothing and where to put it to dry.

Snow
- Soft snow falling on an upturned face.
- Muted sounds as the snow falls.
- Footprints of humans, cats and birds.

- The need for extra layers of clothing, scarves and gloves to keep out the cold.
- The need for boots to keep out wet snow.

Taking this further

Extend vocabulary further to include words like 'waterproof', 'umbrella' and 'snowman'.

Think about why wet washing is put outside only on dry days.

Discuss the way we dress according to the seasons, especially winter and summer (thin/thick clothing; woolly hats/sun hats).

In all weathers, look out for how animals behave.

Walkies!

EYFS aspect	Group size	Resources
Exploration and Investigation Time	Individual	Baby-safe toys – a dog, ball and person

Tell a mini-story using toys as props. Very young children can be propped against cushions, put in a baby bouncer or held on a lap.

* Stimulate the child's interest in the characters to be used before beginning the story.
* Manipulate the characters as the story unfolds:

   Barney is getting very excited because he is going for a walk.
   Jessie puts on his lead and they go out to the park.
   When they are there Jessie throws a ball for Barney who runs after it.
   Barney picks up the ball and brings it back to Jessie.

* The fetching of the ball can continue as many times as you wish.
* Involve the child with the characters and invite her/him to throw the ball for the dog.
* Finish the story with the dog and walker returning home and allow free play with the toys.

> ## Taking this further
>
> A number of scenarios can be enacted with the increasing involvement of the child as she/he develops in manipulative ability – for example, taking a letter to the post, friends going to a party or going on a bus ride.

Strictly Dancing

EYFS aspect	Group size	Resources
Exploration and Investigation ICT Communities	1–2	Tape or CD player (adult or junior version) Variety of music

The CD or tape player is the focus of this activity, but you and a toddler or two will have fun with this dancing session.

- Talk about the pictures on the CD or tape cover and about the music.
- Pick up the toddler and, holding her/him securely, jig about to the rhythm, responding to the changes in the music.
- Pick out the beat by dipping at the knees or tapping gently on the child's back.
- Hold on to the child's hand and do an exaggerated tango together (heads down and sort of charge across the room with outstretched joined hands leading).
- Sing along, be inventive and go with the flow of the music.

This activity can be enjoyed with children from birth upwards, using gentle, swaying music, varying your movements while cradling the baby to suit the mood and tempo of the music. It's also good for soothing and for bedtimes.

You could bounce your own body gently so that the baby feels the rise and fall, or very gently bounce the baby her/himself, although this will not feel so reassuring to the child. You can turn yourself to face different directions as the music changes, so the baby will have a changing view. This might eventually tire her/him so she/he might nod off.

Let the child see as you pause the music and restart the same track and as you stop the music and change the track before moving to the changed rhythm.

Safety note
Ensure that only adults use electrical equipment.

Section 3:
16–26 months

Language development is rapid. Don't forget that most of the activities included in the previous two sections can and should be used with this age group.

Hot and Cold

EYFS aspect	Group size	Resources
Exploration and Investigation	1–4	Magazine pictures of hot and cold things

This will help children to develop a better understanding of familiar hot and cold things.

Preparation
Collect pictures from magazines and catalogues which represent hot and cold. For example:

Cold	*Hot*
Ice cream	Hot dinner
Salad	Fire
Fridge	Cooker
Water	Sun
Snow/ice	Sunny day
Scarf	Iron

Mount them on card or laminate them for future use.

- Lay the pictures out in front of the children and talk about hot and cold sensations. Include warnings about boiling pans on the cooker, hot irons and fires.
- Hold up the cards one at a time for the children to respond with either 'Hot!' or 'Cold!'
- Alternatively, the children could respond with a sharp intake of breath for a hot picture and a shiver for a cold picture.

Doctor, Doctor

EYFS aspect	Group size	Resources
Exploration and Investigation Communities	1–4	'Doctors and nurses' play equipment A doll to take the part of a patient

Introduce the subject of going to the doctors with the rhyme, 'Miss Polly', adding actions:

> *Miss Polly had a dolly who was sick, sick, sick* (cradle doll gently)
> *So they rang for the doctor to be quick, quick, quick* (mime phone)
> *The doctor came with his bag and his hat* (mime holding bag in one hand and tap hat)
> *And he knocked on the door with a rat-a-tat-tat.* (mime knocking on a door)
> *He looked at the dolly and he shook his head* ('examine' doll and shake head)
> *And he said, 'Miss Polly, send her straight to bed'* (wag finger)
> He *wrote on a paper for a pill, pill, pill* (mime writing prescription)
> *'I'll be back in the morning with my bill, bill, bill.* (wave goodbye)

Help the children to 'examine' the doll with whatever toy medical instruments are available, such as a stethoscope or thermometer:

- Take measurements – height and weight.
- Look into the eyes, ears and mouth and take the pulse.
- Finish with a decision on treatment – medicine or putting to bed.

Taking this further

The children themselves can be 'examined' as above as long as the 'patient' is comfortable with what is being checked and they have volunteered.

Old MacDonald

EYFS aspect	Group size	Resources
Exploration and Investigation	1–4	None

Children love to join in with the animal noises of this old favourite.

Old MacDonald had a farm
E-I-E-I-O
And on that farm he had some cows
E-I-E-I-O
With a moo-moo here and a moo-moo there
Here a moo there a moo, everywhere a moo-moo
Old MacDonald had a farm
E-I-E-I-O

For the following verses insert a different animal with its noise. The previous noises can be added to the chorus each time. Make it as long or as short as you like. Other animals to use include:

- ducks/quack-quack
- chickens/cluck-cluck
- sheep/baa-baa
- turkeys/gobble-gobble
- horse/neigh-neigh
- pigs/oink-oink.

Younger children will need a lot of leading and reminding of the order as the chorus grows longer to include all the animals, if you sing the cumulative version.

Phone Errands

EYFS aspect	Group size	Resources
Exploration and Investigation ICT Time	1–2	Toy mobile phone or toy landline set

This game helps the child's understanding of how technology can be used to communicate, and in this case to organize the carrying out of a task.

- Sitting slightly out of sight but still in touch, 'ring' the child's phone and prompt her/him to pick it up and say, 'Hello, it's (Sam) here.'
- Ask Sam a couple of questions, for example whether he's having a happy day, what he had for breakfast.
- Now ask him to carry out an 'important' task, 'Sam, could you please go and see if I remembered to shut the front door/see if the cat is sitting on the table? Can you go and look now, then come back and tell me?' Give as much or as little help as necessary to enable the child to remember the question or task and to give a response via the phone.

Safety note
Ensure that children know the difference between real and toy phones.

> **Taking this further**
> Gradually encourage more independence and confidence with speaking on the phone. Try more complex errands with older and more capable children.

IDEA

32

Keep Moving

EYFS aspect	Group size	Resources
Exploration and Investigation	Individual	None

This is a movement activity which increases awareness of body parts and their names.

Hold the child on your lap facing out or have her/him facing you as you sit or kneel at her/his height. Help the child to hold up each body part as you sing the song slowly. This is sung to the traditional tune, adding body parts for each verse.

One finger, one thumb, keep moving (wiggle finger, then thumb in quick succession)
One finger, one thumb, keep moving (ditto)
One finger, one thumb, keep moving (ditto)
We'll all be merry and bright.
One finger, one thumb, one arm, keep moving (wiggle finger, thumb, lift arm in quick succession. Repeat all as in verse 1)
One finger, one thumb, one arm, one leg, keep moving (add a lift of the leg to other actions and repeat as in verse 1)
One finger, one thumb, one arm, one leg, one nod of the head, keep moving (add a nod of the head).

Taking this further

With older children, add any or all of these:

- **One twist of the ear**
- **One press of the nose**
- **Stand up**
- **Sit down.**

Dolly's Day

EYFS aspect	Group size	Resources
Exploration and Investigation Time Communities	1–4	Any size human doll or soft toy (one between two or one each) Other props, such as play crockery or a doll's blanket

This activity engages children in thinking about daily routines, timescales and sequencing activities.

- Introduce the activity, 'Here's (doll's name). She is just a baby and we're going to look after her.'
- As you talk through the day's events, each child can be allocated a job to help look after the doll – for example, 'Julia, go and tell her to get up now.' 'Tamsyn, wash her face with a flannel.'
- Continue prompts for the imaginary day's activities, such as making her breakfast, going to the park to feed the ducks, having tea and putting her to bed with a story.
- Say 'Goodnight' and relate this to what happens in the children's own routines. Get everyone to softly sing her to sleep with a lullaby, such as 'Twinkle Twinkle Little Star'.

Taking this further

Prompt children to remember all the things they did for the doll in order.

IDEA 34

Memory Cushions

EYFS aspect	Group size	Resources
Exploration and Investigation	Individual	Five small cushions Five different objects to hide under them

This provides an opportunity to develop memory at the same time as introducing and talking about a range of different objects. The objects used here are merely examples and should be varied according to what is available or will be of interest to the child.

- Set out five cushions on the floor or on a sofa. They must be positioned so that they hide objects placed under them.
- Talk about and play with each object in turn before hiding each one under a different cushion. You might use, for example, a toy bus, a ball, a building brick, a soft toy and a toy flute. Make sure the child sees which object goes under which cushion.
- When all the objects are hidden, ask the child to find a particular object.
- Keep going until all the objects have been found. With practice, the discoveries should become less random.

> ## ❗ Taking this further
>
> Try using cushions all the same so that the child has to work out where the object is from position only.
>
> **Try using different colour cushions and asking the child which colour hides each object.**

IDEA 35

Copy It

EYFS aspect	Group size	Resources
ICT	1–2	A home/office photocopier or access to a public copier (at a library or post office)

From an early age children can be involved with pressing buttons under careful guidance. This activity requires access to a black and white photocopier to produce an enlargement of a child's drawing.

- Help the child to produce a simple drawing (no colour at this stage) of, for example, her/himself, Mum, a car or an animal.
- With the child, enlarge the line drawing on a photocopier.
- Help the child to colour the enlarged drawing, keeping the original to compare and contrast with the copy.
- Recap the process with the child, talking about what both the child and the machine did.

Safety note
Reinforce the rule that the children must always have an adult to help them with electrical equipment.

Cue 'Pat-a-Cake'

EYFS aspect	Group size	Resources
ICT Communities	1–4	None

Show the children how to switch on your singing by 'programming' you.

- Make sure all the children know the three cues or triggers that make you sing, i.e. clap hands three times, wiggle fingers in the air, rub tummy.
- Tell the children that every time someone claps you start singing 'Pat-a-Cake'.
- When someone wiggles their fingers in the air, you just can't help singing 'Twinkle Twinkle Little Star'.
- When someone rubs their tummy, you chant, 'Yummy, yummy, yummy, I want food in my tummy.'
- Select one child at a time to clap, wiggle their fingers or rub their tummy and you respond with the allotted action.
- Children can accompany your actions if they understand.

Taking this further

Speed it up a bit.

Swap roles – have a child stand with you facing the other children and invite individuals to clap, wiggle their fingers or rub their tummy to 'program' the standing child.

See if the children can spot you going wrong and needing fixing.

Skittles

EYFS aspect	Group size	Resources
Exploration and Investigation	1–2	Set of skittles with a plastic ball
		Toys which cannot be knocked over

Vary the usual skittles game where a ball is rolled and knocks skittles down to show that not all objects are 'knocked over'.

- Begin with a simple ball-rolling game to gain interest.
- Set up a few light skittles within easy distance and close together.
- Take it in turns to knock down the skittles amid great cheering.
- After a few shots, place one or two small, solid toys among the skittles and have some more target practice.
- Talk about how the skittles are knocked over but the other toys are not.

Feed the Birds

EYFS aspect	Group size	Resources
Exploration and Investigation Time Place	1–4	Art materials Pictures of robins and other garden birds (optional)

This activity focuses children's attention on wildlife and the environment. It is ideally done in winter.

- Discuss winter weather and include what it is like for birds in winter.
- Talk about the need to wear warm clothing.
- Say, sing, and/or teach the words:

Cold fingers
Cold toes
Warm house
Warm clothes
When winter's here we wrap up tight
Against the wind that comes to bite.

Cold ground
Bare trees
Birds cry
Feed us please!
Crumbs and fat and seeds and nuts
Will be a welcome treat for us!

- Look at books to find out what birds need to eat in winter.
- Point out berries and bird tables on walks.
- Children can paint a snowy picture on a blue or dark background with a robin or other birds painted or stuck on.

Safety note
Take care with general hygiene when near bird tables.

Taking this further

Make 'birdcake' out of cake crumbs and nuts, mixed into fat or lard. Help them put it out onto a bird table or similar.

Remember that if you start this, the birds must be fed regularly.

Look at how other animals survive winter.

Press the Button

EYFS aspect	Group size	Resources
Exploration and Investigation ICT	Individual	None

You can make a person into a computer or machine with this simple game.

* Allocate a sound to various body parts, for example a bang to the forehead, a squeak to the ear, a raspberry to the nose, a puff (of air) to the finger.
* Go through each one yourself to demonstrate the idea.
* Invite the child to 'press the buttons' or 'move the levers', with you making the allocated noises as she/he does so.
* Ask the child to take a turn and obtain certain sequences.
* Increase the speed between 'switches'.

Taking this further

Try pushing given parts of the body to cause a reaction from other parts – for example, a push on the nose causes a leg to rise.

Water Wonders

EYFS aspect	Group size	Resources
Exploration and Investigation ICT	1 or 2	Large water tray or sink with safe access Smaller bowl Washing-up liquid Containers of various sizes Water wheel Toys which float and sink Clear plastic two-litre lemonade bottle Empty plastic liquid soap container

Help the children to discover more about water as they play.

Preparation
Carefully cut in half a clear plastic, two-litre lemonade bottle, ensuring that the cut edges are safely smoothed. Make six to ten small holes in the side a little way up from the base. They can be all around the side, but should be at different heights. Any sharp edges on the inside must be smoothed. There will be less of a jagged edge if you use a heated point to pierce the plastic, but take great care! Thoroughly wash out a used liquid soap container, paying special attention to the siphon as soap tends to remain in these. These are some of the things you can do:

- Show how the water flows in jets through the holes in the lemonade bottle (the higher the hole the smaller and weaker the force).
- Use the upper part of the cut lemonade bottle as a funnel to more accurately fill other containers.
- Use the containers to simply fill one from another.
- Talk about the toys which float and sink. See which always float, which float until they are filled with water and which always sink.
- Investigate how the water wheel works. Can you make it go really slowly?
- Fill the liquid soap dispenser with water and investigate how the siphon works.
- Put a little washing-up liquid in a separate, small bowl of water and make a good lather to investigate the bubbles.

Safety note
Keep the washing-up liquid away from the children. Try to ensure that no water is drunk.

Super Sand

EYFS aspect	Group size	Resources
Exploration and Investigation Designing and Making	1–3	Sand tray Toys, including wheeled toys and plastic animals Wheel with buckets

Everyone loves the feel of sand running through their fingers and burying their hands in the sand so this is a good activity purely from the sensory aspect. Help the children to discover more about sand as they play. These are some of the things you can do:

- Investigate how wheeled toys manage or do not manage to go over/through the sand compared to a hard floor.
- Load sand into a truck and move it from one part of the sand tray to another.
- Use a 'water' wheel with buckets. Fill the buckets with sand to make it turn.
- Help to make imaginary stories with toy animals or people hiding in the sand.
- Investigate how sand can be shaken through a plastic bowl sieve.

Section 4:
22–36 months

As children reach three years they make valuable comparisons between much of what they see around them. This allows them to sort and categorize objects and ideas. Remember that most of the activities included in the previous three sections can be used with this age group.

Car Run

EYFS aspect	Group size	Resources
Exploration and Investigation Designing and Making Place	1–4	Wheeled vehicles of different kinds Ramp

Investigate the effect of wheels on a hill.

- Join in a game with cars and suggest making a hill for the vehicles to run down.
- Make a ramp out of cushions and a board.
- Take turns to run vehicles from the top and see how far they go. Encourage the children to simply let go of the vehicle rather than give it a push from the top.
- Compare the different vehicles and how far and fast they travel.
- Alter the height of the ramp to see the effect.

Welcome!

EYFS aspect	Group size	Resources
Time	1–4	Tea set and toy food
Communities		

Set up an imaginary meal with a visitor. This could be incorporated into the normal refreshment break or stand on its own as a game.

- Explain that you have a pretend visitor coming to tea and you want to make them feel very welcome.
- Decide who the visitor is to be. It could be a relative or friend, the nurse from the clinic, a neighbour or the local police officer.
- Decide what the visitor would like to eat and drink and 'prepare' it, giving each child in the group a task.
- When everything is ready, listen to the ring on the doorbell. One of the group can take the part of the visitor or it could be a suitable soft toy or doll.
- Make sure everyone is well mannered during the meal and that the guest is looked after properly.
- During and after the meal there can be pleasant conversation relevant to the choice of visitor.
- At a suitable time, say goodbye to the guest and make sure that everyone helps to clear up.

IDEA
44

Snap Happy

EYFS aspect	Group size	Resources
Time Communities	1–4	Photographs of the children and their families Large sheets of paper Blu-Tack Camera (optional)

This activity helps to put the children in the picture of where they are placed in their family. It relies on how many photographs are supplied by the family and the details they are able to supply with them. Ideally you need some of the children themselves, their brothers and sisters, parents, uncles, aunts and grandparents.

- Have a large sheet of paper for each child and stick a photograph of them in the middle – use Blu-Tack so that the precious snaps can be returned in good condition.
- Take each photograph of the family members in turn and talk about them, assisted as far as possible by the child concerned.
- Point out the similarities where possible – for example, resemblance between brother and sister, curly hair – and enjoy learning more about the child through her/his family. Help the child to understand more about where she/he is in the family group in terms of age.
- Place each photograph in an appropriate position on the sheet, perhaps drawing a line from it to the child in the middle. You could also include your own sheet.
- It is not necessary, but if you have a convenient camera it could be an opportunity – with parental permission – to take a photograph of each child to emphasize the whole process.

What a Day!

EYFS aspect	Group size	Resources
Time Communities	1–4	Large soft toy Any available 'props'

Let the children help you tell a story about Monkey's day (or another animal).

- Have a large cuddly toy on your lap or in the group. In this example it will be Monkey.
- Explain that poor Monkey has forgotten what to do and everyone can help to tell him.
- Encourage the children to help with the details and have props on hand – such as toothbrush, cup, plate, clothing – to help as well.
- Try to use words like 'later', 'before', 'next' and 'last'.
- Essentially the normal daily routines should be covered with any excursions added in, for example:

  - Waking up
  - Breakfast
  - Washing, cleaning teeth and dressing
  - Going out to the park, shops, nursery or playschool
  - Meeting friends
  - Lunch (and maybe a nap)
  - Afternoon activities
  - Going home
  - Teatime
  - Getting ready for bed
  - Going to sleep.

- Remember that for many children, just getting up, cleaning teeth, going to nursery, having tea and going to bed will be enough detail to start with.

Match the Room

EYFS aspect	Group size	Resources
Exploration and Investigation Place	1–4	Shop catalogue Set of building bricks or plastic interlocking bricks Toy people

If there is a large doll's house available it can be used instead of making the rooms out of bricks, but it is not essential.

- Cut out lots of pictures of furniture and equipment found in the home from a shop catalogue.
- Help the children make a set of rooms by laying out brick partitions so that you have, for example, a kitchen, bathroom, bedroom and sitting room. Add one or two small toy people to create reality.
- Talk about the pictures and have the children place them in the correct rooms. Allow for differences in experience among the children for things like ironing boards. Also allow for different names for sitting room, living room, front room or lounge.

Taking this further

You could widen the number of areas to include the garden and even the street.

With older children, try making a chart, sticking sets of 'room' pictures together.

Puzzle Animals

EYFS aspect	Group size	Resources
Exploration and Investigation	1–4	Animal pictures Stiff card Glue

Puzzles are fun to do and concentrate the mind on the details in the picture.

Preparation
Collect large, clear animal pictures and stick them onto rectangles of stiff card. Cut the rectangles – either straight or simply-curved – into three or four pieces. The cuts should divide the animal reasonably equally and produce, if possible, a clear head, middle and rear. Younger children can probably cope with about three puzzles at any one time. Older children may prefer a boxful!

- Share the puzzles, with the pieces mixed up, among the children, giving them two or three different puzzles each. Help them to complete the puzzles, giving hints about the respective features.
- If interest is maintained they can swap their puzzles.

Taking this further
You can increase the degree of difficulty with the puzzle for any really enthusiastic children.

Puzzle People

EYFS aspect	Group size	Resources
Communities	1–4	Pictures of people Stiff card Glue

This is a variation on the puzzle activity in Idea 47.

Preparation
Collect large, clear pictures of people and stick them onto stiff card. There can
be a wide variety of pictures, ideally in a number of 'sets', such as people in
uniform or clothes indicating a clear occupation, and faces of people of
different ages and ethnicities. Cut them out as rectangles or squares, then cut
the shape – either straight or simply-curved – into three or four pieces. The cuts
should divide the person reasonably equally. There is no limit to how many
puzzles you make like this but younger children can probably cope with about
three puzzles at any one time.

- Share the puzzles, with the pieces mixed up, among the children, giving
  them two or three different puzzles each. Help them to complete the
  puzzles, giving hints about the respective features.
- If interest is maintained they can swap their puzzles, but too many at one
  time will be a turn-off.

Taking this further
You can increase the degree of difficulty with the puzzle for any
really enthusiastic children.

Odd One Out

EYFS aspect	Group size	Resources
Exploration and Investigation	1–4	A wide range of toys and easily recognizable objects

Help the children to spot the difference between everyday objects.

- Set up a group of four or five related objects and include one which does not belong in the 'set'.
- Ask the child to pick out the item which does not belong with the others and ask her/him to give a reason for the choice. Welcome all appropriate choices and remember that there may be more than one appropriate answer.
- Repeat with a new set of differently related objects.

Here are some suggestions for the sets:

- A cube among four or five balls.
- A spinning top among four wheeled toys.
- A green ball among some red balls.
- A sock among a number of shoes.
- A wellington boot among three or four training shoes.
- A spoon with three or four forks.
- Something inedible among four food items.
- A plastic item among four things made from paper.

You will see that some of these would be easier to spot than others, so you can choose the groups of objects according to the age and ability of the children. Always ensure a good success rate in order to maintain interest.

Postie!

EYFS aspect	Group size	Resources
Time	1 or 2	Toys related to occupations
Place		Brown paper bags for parcels
Communities		Sticky tape

Become a postal worker and deliver parcels containing tools/equipment to the right places.

- Build with the child an imaginary post van out of suitable furnishings.
- Collect together toys which go with an occupation, such as hammer, stethoscope, spanner, hairdryer.
- Wrap them up as a parcel and 'address' them appropriately, for example Dr Dunn, The Hospital.
- Load all the parcels into the van.
- Set off and deliver each parcel to its address.
- If another child is involved, she/he could be the worker receiving the parcel.

All Day, All Night

EYFS aspect	Group size	Resources
Designing and Making Place Communities	1–4	Cardboard boxes Magazine pictures of animals, including nocturnal animals Art materials, glue Torch

Investigate animals which come out at night.

Cut out animal pictures from wildlife magazines. Stick them onto card so they will stand upright. Put them into two sets:

- daytime animals – garden birds, dogs, horses, squirrels, butterflies, bees
- night animals – rabbits, owls, foxes, hedgehogs, mice, moles, moths.

Work with the children to prepare two cardboard boxes, one to represent daytime and the other, night. The 'day' box should be open at the front and decorated with bright colours, trees, sky (with a sun). This can be done with paint or as a collage. The 'night' box should be closed all round except for a viewing hole at the front and an opening for a torchlight – representing the moon – at the top. The inside of this box should be blackened with paint or paper and decorated with stars. If you cut out silhouettes of houses or trees this will add to the effect.

Once made, these boxes can be used again for similar activities or for repetition.

When all the artwork is set up, talk about the animal pictures and help the children to place them in the correct boxes.

Finally, illuminate the 'night' box with a torch and enjoy looking at the animals in the dark.

Taking this further

Use the boxes for pictures of day and night workers – from emergency services, hospitals, airports, and stations.
Make similar boxes for above-ground and underground animals (worms, moles, rabbits, etc.).
Make similar boxes for land and water creatures.

Town Mouse

EYFS aspect	Group size	Resources
Designing and Making Place Communities	1 or 2	Set of bricks Cardboard boxes Paint and glue Toy cars, traffic lights, etc. Shop catalogues and magazine pictures

Make an imaginary town. You will need a large selection of magazine/catalogue pictures associated with the buildings to go in the town.

- With the help of the children, paint small cardboard cartons to represent key buildings in a town (once painted these can be saved for a similar game another day), for example, hospital/doctors' surgery/clinic, library, school, supermarket and other shops, post office/bank, bus/railway station, factory.
- Place the buildings appropriately within roads lined by toy bricks. Include cars and any traffic paraphernalia available.
- Help the children to place the cut-out pictures in the correct places.
- Ask the children to help you to get a toy figure from A to B and make up a story about the journey.

Safety note
Take the usual safety precautions when using art materials.

Taking this further
If you have a copy, you could read the story *Town Mouse and Country Mouse.*

IDEA

53

Country Mouse

EYFS aspect	Group size	Resources
Designing and Making	1 or 2	Set of bricks
Time		Cardboard boxes
Place		Paint and glue
Communities		Toy farm vehicles and animals
		Magazine pictures of vegetables, milk, cheese, etc.

Make a farm and countryside scene. You will need a large selection of magazine/catalogue pictures associated with the countryside and farms.

• With the help of the children, paint small boxes to represent key buildings on a farm (once painted these can be saved for a similar game another day), for example farmhouse, cattle shed, barns, windmill.

• Place the buildings appropriately within country lanes made from toy bricks. Include toy farm vehicles, if available, and any farm animals.

• Help the children to place the cut-out pictures in the correct places – crops in the arable fields, sheep and cattle in the grassy fields, cows in the cowshed.

• Have the children participate in telling a story about the farm day.

Safety note
Take the usual safety precautions when using art materials.

 Taking this further

If you have a copy, you could read the story *Town Mouse and Country Mouse.*

Kim's Game

EYFS aspect	Group size	Resources
Exploration and Investigation	1–4	Sets of objects or pictures on a theme, e.g. vehicles, baby toys, foods

This popular game develops observation and memory and can be used to focus on a specific subject.

- Present a set of about five related objects or pictures, say vehicles, to the children and talk about them, emphasizing the relationships.
- Explain that you are going to secretly remove just one of the items and they have to work out which one when they look back.
- The children should take turns to spot the missing item in order to give everyone a chance to think clearly.

Taking this further

The children could be asked to help collect the items for the game – this will help to reinforce the concept of sets.

Monday Fun-day

EYFS aspect	Group size	Resources
Time	Any	None

Children will quickly latch on to the rhyming pairs of words and the simple actions to learn painlessly the days of the week.

- *Monday Fun-day* (move flat, outward-facing palms in circles with happy smile)
- *Tuesday Snooze-day* (rest cheek on folded hands)
- *Wednesday Friends-day* (everyone links hands)
- *Thursday Purrs-day* (mime stroking a cat)
- *Friday My-day* (point to yourself)
- *Saturday Chatter-day* (mime chattering to each other or twiddling fingers against the mouth)
- *Sunday Run-day* (run on the spot).

Garden Safari

EYFS aspect	Group size	Resources
Exploration and Investigation	1–4	Specimen containers (optional) Magnifier

This can be done a number of times in the year as the creatures found are seasonal.

- Take the children into a safe garden to look for minibeasts.
- Make sure they know that anything discovered should be protected and not distressed.
- See if they can spot: snails, woodlice, centipedes and beetles under stones, etc.
- With a little more effort they should be able to find: pupae and eggs around tree roots, insects and caterpillars under leaves, spiders in cracks in walls and webs, etc.
- If you collect a few specimens to investigate indoors, use a large magnifier and again remind the children not to cause any distress to the creatures. Do not keep them out of their environment longer than necessary and ensure that the children see you returning them to where they were found.

Safety note
Ensure that the ground covered is safe. Everyone should wash their hands thoroughly immediately after the safari.

Taking this further

Find pictures of some of the creatures in books or on a computer.

Paint a spot on a snail or two so that they can be recognized on a future garden activity.

Find the Fruit

EYFS aspect	Group size	Resources
Exploration and Investigation	1–4	Two of each of a range of vegetables and fruit

This is a match-the-fruit game. The resources can be eaten afterwards or returned to the kitchen for cooking, so care with the handling is essential.

- Cut quite thin slices from the *inside* of several fruits and vegetables, ensuring that the skin or outer layer is removed (for example, a half mushroom will give too much of a clue to the whole vegetable).
- Spread out a range of whole fruits and vegetables, such as banana, orange, apple, pear, kiwi fruit, pepper, cucumber, tomato, mushroom, onion.
- Discuss the foods and their tastes with the children.
- Introduce the inner slices prepared earlier.
- Ask the children to match the slice with its whole fruit.
- You could finish by sharing out the fruit slices.

This is the Way

EYFS aspect	Group size	Resources
Time Place Communities	1–4	Props for the actions (optional)

Practise daily routines and chores to the tune of 'Here We Go Round the Mulberry Bush'.

Help the children to join in the actions and words:

> *This is the way we wash the clothes,* (mime scrubbing clothes in a bowl to rhythm)
> *Wash the clothes, wash the clothes,*
> *This is the way we wash the clothes*
> *And we love to do so.*

> *This is the way we sweep the floor,* (mime sweeping around the room)

> *This is the way we dust the shelves,* (mime dusting)

> *This is the way we wash ourselves,* (mime washing the face)

> *This is the way we dry ourselves,* (mime towel-rubbing movements)

> *This is the way we clean our teeth,* (mime brushing teeth)

Finish with:

> *This is the way we go to sleep,* (mime lying down to sleep)
> *Go to sleep, go to sleep,*
> *This is the way we go to sleep*
> *'Cos we are so tired.*

(alternatively . . . *'Cos we have to do so.*)

Row the Boat

EYFS aspect	Group size	Resources
Time Place Communities	1–4	Kitchen-roll tube 'telescope'

Focus on environments and related events to the tune of 'Row, Row, Row the Boat'.

* Make a 'boat' out of a chair/sofa and cushions.
* Everybody makes rowing movements as they sing the song:

  Row, row, row the boat
  Gently down the stream,
  Looking through my telescope,
  What is this I see?

* Players take it in turns to use the telescope and say what they 'see', repeating the song between each sightseer. You should go first, especially if it is the first time the children have played the game.

Here's an example of how it might go:

You: I see a park
And in that park are trees
And I see a pond with ducks
And I see children playing
They are on the swings and slides.

The children will need prompting in order to come up with a suitable 'sighting', but then their imagination can take it on:

Child (after prompting): I see a supermarket
You: What do you see in the supermarket?
Child: Trolleys
You: What do you see in the trolleys?
Child: Food
You: Who is the food for?
Child: Me!

Ideas for prompts include: a street, my bedroom, the bathroom, the sitting room, playschool.

> ## ❗ *Taking this further*
> The 'sighting' could be a person – Mummy, playleader, garage man, shopkeeper, policeman – and the questions could find out what that person is doing.

Section 5:
30–50 months

Now the children are older and more able to talk about the pictures in books, it is worth remembering the aspects of Knowledge and Understanding of the World while you are looking at them together. Most of the activities included in the previous four sections can be used with this age group.

Sorted!

EYFS aspect	Group size	Resources
Exploration and Investigation	1–4	Various sets of jumbled items as in suggestions

Help children to develop their natural desire to sort things and make sense of what they see. Present the children with a jumbled mixture of items, chosen for what you would like them to sort.

Example 1: sorting balls or bricks for colour
- Start with a short game with coloured balls or bricks before guiding attention to a game of sorting them into colour groups.
- Suggest building separate towers with individually coloured bricks or making a game of rolling, say, the green balls to hit the yellow balls.

Example 2: sorting for shape
- If you have a set of building bricks of different shapes, spread them out and talk about the cubes, triangles and cylinders and any other shape represented.
- Set the challenge to group the various shapes, helping as necessary.
- Finish with building structures using single-shaped bricks.

Example 3: tidying the dressing-up box (if it is always kept tidy, jumble it up for this)
- Ask the children to help sort the clothing into tops, bottoms, shoes, bags, necklaces, scarves, hats or any appropriate categories.
- Finish with a dressing-up game.

Safety note
To avoid choking, beware of small items in any collection.

Taking this further

With older children a large collection of big buttons can be sorted for type. They may also be able to sort toys into wheeled, electric, plastic, wooden, and so on, according to their own ideas.

Build it with Bricks

EYFS aspect	Group size	Resources
Exploration and Investigation Designing and Making	1–4	A clean house brick Self-adhesive address labels Colouring materials, e.g. wax crayons Paper

Add a building element to artwork.

- Talk about house bricks and show the children one. Let them feel it and hold it if you think it is safe for them to do so.
- Take them outside to investigate a brick wall close up, pointing out the patterns made in laying the bricks. Point out, also, the cement between the bricks.
- The artwork can be as simple or elaborate as you like. The object is that the children have an attempt at 'laying' bricks in a traditional pattern using self-adhesive address labels.
- Give the children a number of address labels, depending on the number of children in the group, to colour in various shades of brick red and orange.
- Help them stick the finished labels onto paper in a bricklayer's pattern.
- You could leave the artwork at that or turn it into a picture of Humpty Dumpty or the two little dickie birds sitting on the wall. Complete the house with a door and window or two.

Taking this further

Build a brick wall from interlocking toy bricks.

IDEA
62

Make Music

EYFS aspect	Group size	Resources
Exploration and Investigation Designing and Making	1–4	Empty, washed margarine or ice cream tubs Elastic bands Empty biscuit tin Sturdy cardboard cartons Beaters

Introduce the children to the idea of making music together.

- Set up a range of 'drums' with an upturned margarine or ice cream tub, biscuit tin and a strong cardboard carton (a toy drum can be included if it is available).
- Let the children experiment with the different sounds, using lightweight beaters. Point out the differences between the materials used.
- Take a margarine tub (the 1kg ones are best for this) and stretch up to three large, thick elastic bands across it. Demonstrate the sound made by plucking the elastic bands.
- Rather than allowing the children to play randomly, agree a signal for the various instruments to be struck or plucked individually and compose a 'tune'.
- Include a toy flute or any other toy instrument, if available.

Safety note
Take great care with the elastic bands.

Taking this further
Experiment with stretching the elastic bands to produce higher notes.

Mousey, Mousey

EYFS aspect	Group size	Resources
ICT	Individual	Access to a computer and printer

Show the child how hard copy images can be obtained.

* Sit with the child at a computer and let her/him see how it starts up.
* Go to the computer's clip art files.
* Pass the computer mouse to the child and help her/him select a suitable picture to colour.
* Let the child see you paste the chosen picture onto a document to print.
* Help the child use the mouse to instruct the computer to print.
* Give the printed copy to the child for colouring.

Safety note
Spend only short periods of time at the computer screen with the child.

IDEA
64

Building Site

EYFS aspect	Group size	Resources
Designing and Making Place	1–4	A good set of toy building bricks, including cylindrical (columns) and arch bricks Magazine pictures or a picture book of buildings A copy of *Sleeping Beauty* or similar 'palace' story (optional)

This activity will help the children to see differences in building styles.

- Look at and discuss with the children some pictures of different buildings, either a collection of them from magazines or in a picture book.
- Help the children to make some simple buildings to which they can add appropriate figures and/or vehicles, for example a barn with farmer and animals; a garage with vehicles; a shop with customers.
- Challenge them to make a much more elaborate building, such as a palace, castle, church or temple.
- Finish with a story, for example *Sleeping Beauty*, where such a building is central.

Bridge It

EYFS aspect	Group size	Resources
Designing and Making	1–4	Junk materials
Place		Pictures of bridges
		A copy of *The Three Billy Goats Gruff* (optional)

Introduce the idea of a bridge in a practical way.

- Show and discuss pictures of bridges with the children.
- Set the challenge to make a bridge to span, say, two cushions.
- Talk about the junk materials to be used. Particularly useful for this are the long card tubes from the cores of kitchen roll and gift wrapping paper (they can be joined by squashing one end and pushing it inside another, rather than using glue or tape). You could also use flat card from, for example, the sides of cereal boxes.
- Help the children as little as possible with their constructions so that they can solve the problems themselves.
- Encourage them to build a strong bridge. They will need more help if they want to stick or tape pieces together.
- When the bridges are finished, tell or read the story of *The Three Billy Goats Gruff*.
- Finish with a big tidy-up.

Taking this further

Make a tunnel to use with a train set.

Make a miniature bridge in the garden for snails and other creatures to cross.

IDEA 66

Gone Fishing

EYFS aspect	Group size	Resources
Designing and Making Place Communities	1–4	Cut-out fish shapes Giant metal paper clips or paper fasteners String Magnets Short sticks

This game is an old favourite.

Preparation

Cut out several fish shapes – about hand-size – from card. You will need about two or three per child. Make one 'fishing rod' per child using a short (not sharp) stick with a length of string tied to one end. Securely tie a magnet (the bait) to the other end of the string – a ring magnet is ideal as they are stronger, but a small horseshoe magnet or even a fridge magnet will work. The fish's 'mouth' will be either a giant paperclip or a paper fastener. The paper clip is easier and makes a larger target, but it is heavier and weak magnets may not be so effective. If you use paper fasteners, these should be inserted safely into the fish and the prongs taped over.

- Help the children colour the fish in bright colours.
- Make a boat using cushions and sofa/chairs.
- Spread the fish around the boat.
- Climb into the boat with all the fishermen and their rods.
- Take the boat out on a 'rough sea' before stopping to start the fishing.
- The children then 'catch' the fish with the magnets on their rods.
- You could add to the fun by making one of the fish a 'lucky' catch by marking it in some way.

Taking this further

If you live near the sea or where people fish regularly, take the children on a visit.

Bread

EYFS aspect	Group size	Resources
Exploration and Investigation Communities	1–4	Bread slices Corn or wheat stalks or something to represent them Raisins to represent seeds Flour Soft toys A copy of *The Little Red Hen* (optional)

This is based on the *The Little Red Hen* story. It can be done at any time but it is an ideal Harvest Festival introduction. The toys in this case are: Bear, Dog, Duck and Monkey, but they can of course be any which are handy, and you don't have to use four.

- Tell the story, using the toys and other props at the appropriate times. The main elements are here but it should be animated as much as possible for enjoyment.

  One day Bear found some wheat seeds. He wanted to plant them and so he asked for help. 'Who will help me plant these seeds?' he said.

  'Not I,' said Dog. 'Not I,' said Duck. 'Not I,' said Monkey.

  So Bear planted the seeds all by himself. It took a long time. Then Bear saw the weeds growing between the seeds. 'Who will help me to weed the garden?' he said.

  'Not I,' said Dog. 'Not I,' said Duck. 'Not I,' said Monkey.

  So Bear did all the weeding himself. When the wheat grew into tall stems, Bear asked, 'Who will help me to harvest the wheat?' The same replies came.

  'Not I,' said Dog. 'Not I,' said Duck. 'Not I,' said Monkey.

  So Bear cut all the wheat himself and then asked, 'Who will help me to take the wheat to the miller?'

  'Not I,' said Dog. 'Not I,' said Duck. 'Not I,' said Monkey.

  So Bear took the wheat to the miller who ground it into flour. Bear took the flour home and made it into bread. 'Who will help me to eat this bread?' Bear asked when it came fresh from the oven.

'I will!' said Dog. 'I will!' said Duck. 'I will!' said Monkey.

And what did Bear say?

- It's up to you to decide if the others get nothing (as in *The Little Red Hen* story) or if Bear lets them off after they promise to help next time. The children might like to be part of that decision.
- Finish with a little feast of the bread and any unused raisins.

IDEA 68

Noah's Ark

EYFS aspect	Group size	Resources
Exploration and Investigation Designing and Making Communities	1–4	A sticker book of animals or magazine pictures of animals Sheets of paper Glue stick if necessary

Preparation

Build your own Noah's Ark and fill it with animals as you tell the story. Make sure you have plenty of animal pictures, either cut out from magazines or, ideally, from an animal sticker book. They will need to be stuck onto large pieces of paper, so have them ready.

- Introduce the story of Noah's Ark and how two of each animal in the world were saved from the flood.
- 'Build' an ark, using the available furnishings such as a sofa surrounded by cushions – something that everyone can get into off the floor.
- Explain that you now have to find pairs of all the animals. Talk about the different animals as they are found.
- When everything is ready, listen for the rain, then pack your things and all the animals into the Ark.
- Ride out the storm safely until the doves find land.
- When you arrive on dry land set all the animals free.

Safety note
Take great care if moving items of furniture or large cushions.

Butterflies

EYFS aspect	Group size	Resources
Designing and Making Place	1–4	Liquid paints Sugar paper Butterfly pictures

This is a good art activity for the summer when the butterflies are about.

- Fold sheets of sugar paper in half.
- On the centre crease, mark out a butterfly body, head, wings and antennae with a felt marker pen.
- Set the context by looking at butterfly pictures with the children. If it is the right time of year, go into the garden and look for some butterflies.
- With everything and everybody suitably protected for an art activity, demonstrate the technique. Using two or three different-coloured liquid paints, make a simple pattern on one side of the sheet of paper.
- Fold the second half onto the wet paint and press down all over.
- Open carefully to show the symmetrical pattern of merged colours.
- Set it aside to dry.
- Help the children with their own pieces.
- When dry, cut round the felt marker wing shapes to make the finished butterfly.

All Dressed Up

EYFS aspect	Group size	Resources
Exploration and Investigation Communities	1–4	Lots of dressing-up clothes made from different materials

Dressing-up is something all children love to do and there are many opportunities to direct their thoughts to the concepts involved with clothing. Here are a few suggestions.

- Look at the various materials used. Help the children to recognize the differences in feel and weight between wool, felt, cotton, silk, lace and plastic.
- Help them sort the clothes into colours, tops and bottoms.
- Look at different kinds of shoes and talk about who would wear them.
- Hats have great potential. They are quite easy to make or to decorate and can transform the wearer dramatically into anyone they want to be. Any hats connected to a uniform, for example, will enable a child to get right into character.
- Relate the various outfits you have to people the children know.

Taking this further

Why not organize a fancy dress parade or a funny hat competition?

The Enormous Turnip

EYFS aspect	Group size	Resources
Exploration and Investigation Place Communities	1–4	A copy of *The Enormous Turnip* (optional) A turnip, swede, cabbage or any other suitable vegetable Cuddly toys

Enact the old favourite story. This activity is more suitable for the upper end of this age range and works very well far beyond.

You do not actually need a copy of the story because the idea is very simple and to enact it you will need to change the characters according to what you have available. However, you could start by reading the story first and changing it with the children afterwards.

The general idea is that a gardener grows an enormous turnip, which is so big he cannot pull it up by himself. He calls on his wife to help and on progressively smaller characters as the job is still not done. Eventually the tiniest creature (usually a mouse) is enough to complete the task. They cook the turnip and all sit down to eat it.

The involvement of the children will depend on their stage of development. These are the suggested points to follow when acting out the story:

- Begin with introducing the turnip (or other large vegetable), elaborating as much as you like on how it is cooked and what it tastes like.
- Introduce the 'gardener', who is an appropriate soft toy.
- Show the gardener planting seeds, watering and weeding to grow the turnip.
- Show the gardener very pleased and proud of his work and on the growth of the turnip.
- Show the gardener struggling to pull it up.
- Call for a number of different soft toys in turn, each one smaller or weaker than the one before, making them form a chain, each pulling on the one in front.
- Finally, make the smallest toy able to cause the pull that removes the turnip.
- Have all the characters taking the turnip into the house, cooking it and eating it.

Taking this further

With a group of children they themselves could be the characters and perhaps use just one cuddly toy at the end to make the difference. Take great care at the final tug and avoid children tumbling on top of each other.

Leaf Prints

EYFS aspect	Group size	Resources
Exploration and Investigation Designing and Making Place	1–4	Liquid paint Sugar paper Leaves

Investigate leaf shapes through art.

- Collect a wide range of fallen leaves. Do this with the children if the trees are conveniently nearby.
- Rinse the leaves in a bowl of water and spread them out on some newspaper or a towel.
- Talk about the shapes, structure and colours.
- Once everything is suitably protected against what will be a messy art activity, demonstrate the technique.
- Thickly cover a chosen leaf with liquid paint; turn it over to print onto a piece of paper; repeat the printing to make a pattern. A further effect can be achieved by overlaying different colours.
- Now let the children do it!

Safety note
Take normal hygiene precautions.

Right up your Street

EYFS aspect	Group size	Resources
Exploration and Investigation Place	1–2	None

There is a great deal to discover and talk about in an ordinary street.

Take the children out into a safe nearby street. Any street, anywhere, will have something interesting that the children may not have noticed before. Point out to them some of the following:

- Street signs – the name of the street itself, traffic warnings/directions.
- Front gardens of the houses and any other interesting features they have.
- Drains and other signs of underground workings – hydrants and telephone inspection covers.
- The natural world of the street – trees and bushes, flowers, birds and other animals.
- Safe ways to cross the road – taking into account the pavement, kerb and any traffic islands or crossings and any parked or moving vehicles.

Remind the children of the dos and don'ts:

- Do look where you are going/Don't cross the road on your own.
- Do look after the street/Don't drop litter.
- Do stay on the pavement/Don't go into other people's gardens.

Bobo's House

EYFS aspect	Group size	Resources
Designing and Making	1–3	Junk materials and card
Place		Art materials
		A cuddly toy (Bobo)

This is a fun session of making things.

- Ask the children to choose a cuddly toy and make a home for it.
- Help them select suitable junk materials to build a one- or two-room house and include furnishings such as a table and chairs, cupboards and a bath.
- When it is finished, encourage the children to move their cuddly toy (for example, Bobo) in and around the home and make up little stories about what happens and what he does – 'Bobo got up in the morning and had a bath. He sat at the table and had his breakfast. He went out into the garden.'

Alternatively, go for a smaller-scale home inside a shoebox or similar-sized container for a toy figure.

- Cut a main door in the side of the box.
- Divide the box into two or three rooms with card partitions. Cut doors into the walls first and then the partitions can be fixed into the box with a stapler (as long as you keep it away from the children).
- Help the children to make furniture, using small junk items and folded card. It may be as elaborate as their ability and patience will allow.
- When it is finished, encourage the children to use it for an imaginative game as above.

Safety note
Take the usual precautions when using art materials. Take care with very small 'junk' items like bottle tops. Cover any staples with tape.

IDEA
75

Baby Animals

EYFS aspect	Group size	Resources
Exploration and Investigation	1–4	Pictures of puppies, kittens, etc.
ICT		Internet access
Time		A copy of *The Ugly Duckling*
Place		

The children will enjoy finding out about baby animals – and so will you.

- Tell the story of *The Ugly Duckling* and talk about how animals look different and behave differently when they are young, for example frogs and tadpoles, cats and kittens.
- Show pictures of as many young animals you can find – puppies, kittens, calves, lambs, piglets, chicks.
- Before working with the children, locate a path to pictures and clips of young animals through a search engine for images on the internet. Let the children see and 'help' you navigate.

IDEA 76

Nesting

EYFS aspect	Group size	Resources
Exploration and Investigation Designing and Making	1–4	Brown liquid paint Paper plates Masking tape Art straws Crushed dry leaves and other plant material Toy bird, e.g. a duck

Make a home for a toy bird.

Preparation
Make some paper plates a little more bowl-shaped by making short cuts towards the centre at regular intervals around the outside. Overlap the edges of the cuts and tape with masking tape. Cut flattened art straws into lengths of approximately 3cm. Then make up a mixture of brown liquid paint and white PVA glue.

- Begin by talking about and looking at pictures of animal homes and how you might make them.
- Concentrate on birds' nests, remembering that not all bird species build nests and they are not all in trees.
- Introduce the toy bird who needs to build a home, and set the challenge to make one.
- Help the children to thickly paint the prepared paper nest shapes with the paint/glue mixture.
- Overlap 'twigs' (the art straw lengths) in the wet paint and lightly brush more paint over the top.
- Press down bits of dry leaves and thin plant stems on top as 'bedding' and leave to dry.
- Make up a little story of how the toy managed to build its nest and settle it in.

IDEA
77

Bobo's Birthday

EYFS aspect	Group size	Resources
Time Communities	1–4	Cuddly toy (Bobo) Wrapping paper and tape Toy tea set 'Cake' with a birthday candle

Establish time order with a birthday.

- Ask the children to imagine it is the cuddly toy's (Bobo's) birthday and relate it to their own birthdays and the birthdays of those close to them.
- Involve them in the discussion about what they can give as presents – small toys from somewhere in the room.
- Help the children to wrap the presents they have chosen.
- 'Wake' Bobo and wish him 'Happy Birthday!'
- Give the presents and help Bobo to unwrap them with appropriate drama.
- Get Bobo ready to go out for an imaginary birthday treat. This could be simply a walk in the park to feed the ducks or anything you or the children think of.
- Sit everyone down for 'tea', with Bobo in the seat of honour.
- Present Bobo with a birthday cake and candle. Decide whether or not you are going to light the candle. This can be a small individual-sized cake. The rest of the birthday tea can be a fruit snack for the children.
- Sing 'Happy Birthday'.
- Help the children and Bobo to eat the cake. Everyone will have just a very small piece.
- Play a short, two-minute game, such as hide and seek, after tea.
- Put Bobo to bed.
- Go through the 'day' with the children, asking them to try to remember what happened and the order in which it all happened.

IDEA 78

Mouldy Bread and Cheese!

EYFS aspect	Group size	Resources
Exploration and Investigation Time	1–4	Transparent plastic container with lid Slices of bread A thin slice of cheese

This activity shows what can happen to food if we do not keep it fresh.

- Begin by talking about bread, perhaps at snack time when bread is available to eat.
- Explain that fresh bread is good but if you keep it too long it can go bad, as can all other food. Talk about the need for fridges to keep food fresh.
- Take a slice or half-slice of bread and a piece of cheese and put them in a transparent plastic container.
- Explain that you are going to leave them in the container in the warm room and watch each day to see what happens.
- Enjoy the rest of the snack with the children.
- In preparation for later inspections of the decaying samples over the days to come make lots of small holes in the container lid so that air can circulate.
- Seal the lid on the container so that the children cannot remove it and investigate too closely.
- Look together at the samples each day and discuss what happens to the bread and cheese.

 Taking this further

You could try samples of other foods – such as milk or cabbage – as long as the resulting smell is not too obtrusive.

IDEA 79

Winging It

EYFS aspect	Group size	Resources
Exploration and Investigation	1–4	Pictures of winged creatures Card and glue

Make a wing puzzle.

Preparation
Stick pictures of winged animals in flight onto card. Cut out the animals, then cut one wing from each and put them in a box.

Suggested animal groups include birds (garden birds, swans, geese, eagles), insects (bees, dragonflies, butterflies), bats, fantasy creatures (dragons).

- Begin by looking at a picture book of flying creatures or a story about birds or dragons.
- Show the winged animal cards and their removed wings (mixed up together) and challenge the children to complete the creatures.
- Help to ensure the correct wings are placed to complete the set.
- Consolidate the activity by having a bit of fun seeing what they would look like with the wrong wings.

IDEA
80

Circle Animals

EYFS aspect	Group size	Resources
Exploration and Investigation	1–4+	None

This is a game of animal miming.

- Sit in a large circle with the children.
- Talk about animal sounds and movements, such as a lion's roar and pounce, a horse's neigh and gallop.
- Begin with sounds. You will need to demonstrate at first and then get the children to repeat it.
- Go around the group in turn, allocating an animal to each person, beginning with yourself:

    I am going to be a . . . mouse (squeak like a mouse)
    Cassie, you can be a . . . cat (Cassie mews like a cat)
    Damien, you can be a . . . cow (Damien moos)
    Alfie, you can be a . . . sheep (Alfie bleats)
    Jasmine, you can be a . . . dog (Jasmine barks).

- After one or two rounds, demonstrate the movements of some animals.
- Go around the group in turn again – beginning with yourself – but this time each person gets up and goes around the circle in the style of the animal allocated to them. The children could be invited to choose your animal.

    I am going to be an . . . elephant (stomp heavily around the circle with arm/trunk swinging and return to your place)
    Cassie, you can be a . . . horse (Cassie gallops round and back to place)
    Damien, you can be a . . . rabbit (Damien bunny hops around)
    Alfie, you can be a . . . kangaroo (Alfie jumps around)
    Jasmine, you can be a . . . snake (Jasmine slithers around, but be careful of carpet burn!).

- Be prepared to give lots of encouragement to less confident children and, if necessary, let them sit out and watch.

Face Up to It

EYFS aspect	Group size	Resources
ICT Communities	1–4	Pictures of faces Digital camera Access to a computer

Concentrate on a wide selection of faces to inspire conversation.

Preparation
Collect as wide a variety of photographs of faces as you can to include:

- young and old
- male and female
- all skin colours and ethnicities
- interesting facial expressions
- interesting hairstyles.

There are a number of published posters and books available, but magazines are also a good source.

- Talk to the children about faces, how we recognize people and the ways people customize their appearance – hairstyle, beards, make-up.
- Show the picture collection and invite the children to talk about the characters. The spontaneous responses of the children are likely to show great insight but, if you feel they need directing, choose a few photographs and ask specific questions about the people, for example 'Does he have a kind face? Happy face? Glasses? Beard?'
- Give each child two or three photographs and ask each child in turn to tell the group something about one of their photographs, such as, 'The lady is wearing a lovely hat.' The children will need lots of prompts with this.
- Repeat until all the selected photographs have been described in some way.
- Show the children that their faces, too, can be photographed so they can see themselves as others see them. If you have parental permission, take digital photographs of the children's faces and/or the faces of any familiar adults available. Let the children see you download them onto a computer and enjoy seeing themselves appear on the screen. Help them click through the images.
- Alternatively, if there is no parental permission for photographs, let the children use a mirror to study their own facial features and talk about what they see.

Turning Over a New Leaf

EYFS aspect	Group size	Resources
Exploration and Investigation Time	1–4	A large selection of different types of leaves at various stages of decay.

This activity is best done at the beginning of autumn when there are plenty of freshly fallen leaves but still, also, green leaves on the trees.

- Collect fallen leaves of different trees from the area. This can be done with the children.
- If there are still some trees with leaves that have not yet 'turned' then pick a few of those as well. Broad-leaved evergreens will do fine but *not* holly.
- Search especially for older leaves, i.e. partially-eaten leaves and leaf skeletons (those with only the veins left).
- Rinse the leaves in plenty of water, sieve them and spread them out to dry.
- When dry, lay the leaves out for the children to sort.
- Help them see the differences in colour, size and shape and degree of decay.

Safety note
Hands should be washed after handling organic material.

 Taking this further

You could make charts by sticking some of the leaves onto sugar paper, selected for special colouring or as a timeline, graduating from fresh to skeleton.

Try pressing some of the more attractive specimens in a flower press.

What's My Line?

EYFS aspect	Group size	Resources
Communities	1–4	Lots of dressing-up clothes Toy tools and accessories

Organize a dressing-up parade based on different occupations.

- Talk to the children about jobs people do and any special clothing they may wear – uniforms, hard hats, aprons, boiler suits.
- If you have any toy tools or instruments – for example, hammer, saw, stethoscope – talk about who would use them and how they are used.
- Ask the children to dress as 'workers', giving any necessary direction depending on availability of clothing. Help the children to decide and encourage them to find accessories which make the overall effect more accurate. The more they can manage this themselves the better, but they will need direction. The learning is in the decision making.
- Once everyone is ready, arrange a fancy-dress parade, including any acting of the occupations the children may wish to do.
- You could award stickers or similar 'prizes' to winners, ensuring that everyone receives one for some part of their costume.

Section 6:
40–60+ months

Children at this age develop logical thinking. The richness of the experiences they have already encountered combines with sophisticated language and social skills to enable them to solve problems. Encourage the children to ask questions about everything they see and do. Remember that many of the activities included in the previous five sections can be used with this age group.

Balloons: Up and Away

EYFS aspect	Group size	Resources
Exploration and Investigation Designing and Making	1–4	Assorted balloons Balloon pump

Have fun investigating air pressure and jet propulsion.

Most children by this age will have seen inflated balloons and will know they can burst suddenly but just in case, it will be necessary to carry out a 'controlled explosion':

- Inflate a balloon.
- Talk about balloons and where the children have seen them.
- Hold the inflated balloon carefully and explain that the air wants to get out. If the balloon is broken, say with a pin, or sat on it will burst with a loud bang.
- Tell the children it would not hurt, but it is very sudden and a bit of a shock.
- Prepare them by explaining that you are going to burst the balloon. Do so when they are ready.
- Remind them that the 'bang' is the air escaping very fast.

Inflate a single balloon and hold the neck without tying it off, then demonstrate:

- how air escapes with a loud hiss when you release your grip just a little, letting them feel the escape of air gently on their faces or backs of their hands
- how air escapes with a high-pitched squeak when the neck is stretched as the air escapes
- how the balloon shoots off noisily when let go.

Inflate a few balloons and let the children play with them together, as long as none have sharp fingernails. To build awareness of how air-filled balloons move, try some of these games:

- 'How long can we keep a balloon in the air?' – everyone flicks it upwards as it nears them.
- Simply pass the balloon between two or three children.
- Throw a long 'sausage' balloon, spear-like, at a target.

Encourage the children to ask questions about what they have seen and done.

Safety note
Make sure that this activity is closely controlled. Balloon inflation should be done by adults only. Children can become very excited with balloons.

Taking this further

You can demonstrate controlled jet propulsion quite easily, but it may need more than one pair of adult hands:

- Thread a long piece of string through a straw and suspend it across the room.
- Inflate a long 'sausage' balloon and insert a cork with a hole in it (about 1mm diameter) in the neck, keeping a finger over the hole.
- Use masking tape to attach the balloon to the straw.
- Let go of the balloon and watch it sail across the room. The speed will depend on the size of hole in the cork.

With a set of specially shaped balloons, try making animals or twisting them into designs.

IDEA

85

Balloons:
Static Electricity

EYFS aspect	Group size	Resources
Exploration and Investigation	1–4	Balloons Balloon pump Woolly jumper

Have fun investigating static electricity.

It is advisable to run through this experiment yourself before showing the children, just in case the woolly jumper you use is not so effective. The closer the fabric is to real wool the better.

- It's a good idea to first carry out a 'controlled explosion', as described in Idea 84, to show children how balloons can burst suddenly.
- Inflate a balloon and show how it falls to the ground when you let it go.
- Hold it against a flat wall and let it go so the children see that it falls in the same way.
- 'Charge' the balloon with electricity by rubbing it rapidly on a woolly jumper, preferably one you are wearing.
- Hold the balloon against the wall and see that it now 'sticks' there.
- The children will find it difficult to charge the balloons themselves and there could be a few bursts if you let them, but charge as many balloons as you can for the children to try before your arm becomes too tired.

Safety note
Make sure that this activity is closely controlled. Balloon inflation should be done by adults only. Children can become very excited with balloons.

Taking this further

Static electricity can also be demonstrated in the following ways:

- Small pieces of tissue paper will be attracted to a 'charged' plastic comb (rubbed on woollen material).
- A steady stream of water from the tap (as slow as possible without breaking up) will 'bend' towards a 'charged' ballpoint pen barrel held alongside it.

IDEA 86

Chasing Shadows

EYFS aspect	Group size	Resources
Exploration and Investigation	1–4	None

Investigate shadows outdoors.

- Choose a sunny day and go outside into a safe open space, preferably earlier or later in the day when shadows are longer.
- Point out the shadows formed on the ground and explain, 'We are standing in the way of the sunlight.'
- With their backs to the sun, have the children look at their shadows and then try to tread on them.
- Suggest they move around in all directions and watch their shadows lead, follow or go alongside them.
- Look at the shadows formed by natural and built structures nearby.
- If it is warm as well as sunny, find some shade, sit down and have a story, reminding the children that they should not spend too long in the sun.

Safety note
Make sure that no one looks directly at the sun. Do not spend too long in strong sunlight.

Me and My Shadow

EYFS aspect	Group size	Resources
Exploration and Investigation	1–4	Projector or strong torch Large sheets of white or pale sugar paper Black sugar paper Marker pen Coloured pencils/crayons

Investigate shadows indoors.

- Set up a strong light source to shine onto a plain wall. An overhead projector is ideal. If using a different projector or large torch, ensure that the children do not look directly into the light.
- Have some fun making shadow pictures on the wall with hands.
- Fix a large sheet of white sugar paper to the wall in the 'spotlight'.
- Ask a child to stand sideways in front of the light so that the shadow of their head is shown in profile on the paper.
- Carefully draw around the shadow with a marker pen. Repeat this with the other children.
- When every shadow has been drawn, turn off the light source.
- Fasten each drawn profile to a sheet of black sugar paper.
- Carefully cut both sheets around the outline to give two heads.
- The children can colour the white copy as a self-portrait and the black one is its shadow.

Safety note
No one should look directly into the light source. Make sure the children do not touch the projector and warn them that it gets hot.

IDEA

88

What Do You Feel?

EYFS aspect	Group size	Resources
Exploration and Investigation	1–4	Large cardboard box A range of small objects with distinctive shapes or textures

Put a little mystery into investigating shape and texture.

- Seal the flaps of a large cardboard box. Cut a hole in one side, large enough for a hand and arm to go in and move around. Cover the box with black paper and decorate it.
- Put four or five objects in the box without the children seeing.
- Challenge each child in turn to put in their hand, take hold of an object and say what it is without bringing it out or looking at it.
- As they are feeling the object, encourage them to talk about what it feels like. Ask questions about the feel – Is it soft? Is it shiny? Is it a square shape? Is it round?
- Once a guess is given, ask them to bring it out to see if the guess was right.
- Once an object has been guessed, whether correctly or incorrectly, keep it out of the box.
- Objects to try include: small fruits (orange, apple, banana), balls (vary the kinds), cotton wool, plastic or rubber ring, keys, familiar toys made of plastic, rubber, wood, metal and stuffed fabric.

IDEA
89

What's That Smell?

EYFS aspect	Group size	Resources
Exploration and Investigation	1–4	Small plastic food pots with lids Range of substances with distinctive smells

Concentrate the mind on some aromas.

Preparation
Select some powders and liquids with quite strong distinctive smells, for example:

- Liquids: soap, vinegar, perfume, orange juice
- Powders: curry, talcum powder, coffee, washing powder, herbs.

Place a little of each substance in a transparent plastic container. Make pinholes in the lids (this can be done more easily with a hot needle). Tape the lids firmly onto the containers so that they will not come open and spill the contents.

- With the children in a group, talk about how we use the nose to smell.
- Show the pots. Reinforce the warnings about tasting unknown liquids and powders and explain that all these are safely sealed in the pots.
- Take each pot in turn and say what is inside.
- Let each child take a good sniff and say what they think about it.
- Encourage the children to say which is their favourite/least favourite smell among the samples.

Safety note
Ensure that the containers remain sealed throughout the activity.

Taking this further
Older children may like to do this as a guessing game.

Flower Power

EYFS aspect	Group size	Resources
Exploration and Investigation	1–4	A range of flowers
Time		Sugar paper
Place		Flower press (optional)
Communities		

This hands-on look at flowers can be done at almost any time of year but it is better in the warmer months when there is a wider range of blooms available.

- Show a bunch of flowers which includes a lot of different colours and flower heads.
- Talk about the fragrance, colour, petals, leaves and stem and the feel-good factor of flowers.
- Discuss where and when the children have seen cut flowers used – for example, at home, in places of worship, as gifts for birthdays and anniversaries and on cards, at weddings and other special occasions.
- Explain the seasonal nature of flowers' growth and the importance of insects.
- Go outside and look at flowers in the garden or in a nearby park. Point out wild flowers like daisies and buttercups, as well as the cultivated ones.
- Let the children pick a few common wild flowers, impressing on them that only some flowers should be picked while most should be left to grow and look beautiful.
- Help them carefully to sandwich their flower collections between two pieces of sugar paper.
- Place in a flower press and screw down tightly. Alternatively, weigh down with several large books.
- After a few days, remind the children what they did with the flowers and give them the pressed samples as keepsakes.

Safety note
Safeguard children with pollen allergies and remember that pollen can stain clothing.

Taking this further

Use the pressed flowers in artwork to make a card for a relative who likes flowers.

Sow the Seeds

EYFS aspect	Group size	Resources
Exploration and Investigation Time	1–4	Cress seeds Runner bean seeds Shallow dishes Transparent plastic tumblers Food-safe kitchen roll

Grow some plants from seed. Cress grows more quickly than beans and can be eaten. Runner beans take longer but allow the root to be seen, although it cannot be eaten.

Talk to the children about how seeds grow into plants. Explain that although plants normally grow in the soil, some can be grown on wet tissue paper as well because they have light, water and food from the seed. Work with the children to 'plant' the seeds, allowing them to do as much of the task as they are able.

For cress seeds:

- Place a thick pad of food-safe kitchen roll in a shallow dish.
- Moisten it so that it just lays flat.
- Spread the cress seeds evenly over the kitchen roll.
- Add more water to the side of the dish so that it is soaked up by the kitchen roll but the seeds are not disturbed.
- Place the dish in a warm, safe place for observing over the coming days. Germination is quicker in the dark but there needs to be light as soon as the shoots appear.
- Add water to the side of the dish daily, just enough to keep the kitchen roll wet without flooding.
- The seeds will germinate within a few days.
- When grown to about 3cm, the cress can be cut with scissors and eaten as a salad.
- Make sure the children know that, although cress is edible, not all plants are and some can be harmful.

For runner bean seeds, show the children the seeds inside a runner bean so that they realize where they come from. Make sure they know that the runner beans are edible but the plant itself is not.

- Line a transparent plastic tumbler with a thick pad of food-safe kitchen roll, allowing a space in the middle for watering.
- Wedge one or two runner bean seeds between the kitchen roll and side of the tumbler, about 3cm up from the bottom, so that they can be clearly seen through the plastic.
- Pour a little water into the middle of the tumbler so that it is soaked up in the kitchen roll.
- You may have to add more kitchen roll and readjust the beans at this point.
- Place the tumbler in a warm, safe place for observing over the coming days.
- Add water to the tumbler daily, just enough to keep the kitchen roll wet without flooding.
- Roots should begin to emerge in a few days or a week and grow quite quickly. The shoot will take longer to be recognizable.
- If you leave this plant long enough you should be able to see some leaves before it outgrows the tumbler. The root growth by then will be quite considerable.

Remember to let the children help with the daily watering whenever possible. Discuss the growth observed whenever you can.

Safety note
Keep all seeds away from the mouth.

Taking this further

If it is the right time of year, a healthy runner bean plant can be transplanted into soil in a pot or corner of the garden. Add a cane and the children can see how it climbs, flowers and produces beans. Look out for the bees playing their part as well.

IDEA

92

Recording!

EYFS aspect	Group size	Resources
Exploration and Investigation ICT Place Communities	1–4	Tape recorder

Play a game of 'Guess the Sound'.

- Make a recording of as many familiar sounds as possible, each up to about ten seconds' duration. Allow a few seconds between each sound to facilitate pausing. Try recording sounds such as a washing machine and other kitchen appliances, traffic, mobile phone ring tones, familiar voices, a motorcycle engine, 'noisy' familiar toys and splashing/running water.
- Have the children listen carefully as you play the recording from beginning to end.
- Tell them that they now have to guess what each sound is when you play them one at a time.
- Pause the machine after each sound to allow the guesses, giving clues for any which prove difficult.
- You can make your own rules for a quiz-type competition if you wish, or keep it simple. Ensure that those children who are slower to answer have a chance to be successful as well.

Safety note
Take the usual care when using mains electricity equipment.

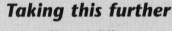

Taking this further

A recording of different sound effects, available from shops and, sometimes, the local lending library, will contain much more varied (and more difficult) sounds.

IDEA

93

What's That?

EYFS aspect	Group size	Resources
Exploration and Investigation ICT Place	1–4	Digital camera Access to a computer

This game looks at familiar objects from unusual angles. It can be done from prints obtained from an older-style film camera, such as a disposable one, but the picture quality for close-up is often not so good.

- Take digital photographs of familiar objects or areas at unusual angles – from directly above, directly below, close up, at a corner, something closed when normally open or open when normally closed, a small part of a large object. Ideas for objects include a washing machine and other kitchen appliances, furniture, a familiar toy, garden features, plants and trees, or parts of the outside of the building, such as a drainpipe. You could also photograph parts of the room in which the game is played and patterns on the furnishings in the room.
- Download the photographs onto a computer.
- Show one or two objects to the children and point out how they look at different angles.
- Show them some or all of the pictures on the computer and explain how you made them.
- Allowing the children to move between the pictures as much as possible, show each in turn and ask the children to guess what they are, giving clues for any which prove more difficult.
- You can make your own rules for a quiz-type competition if you wish, or keep it simple. Ensure that those children who are slower to answer have a chance to be successful as well.

Safety note
Take the usual precautions when using mains electrical equipment.

Taking this further

Involve the children in taking some photographs at unusual angles of familiar adults (who have volunteered), for example a back view of the head, ear and shoulder or a particularly distinctive area which has a piece of jewellery or a tattoo.

Clues from the Past

EYFS aspect	Group size	Resources
Time Place Communities	1–4+	Photographs and toys of historical interest (see below)

Learn about the past through toys.

- Make a collection of photographs of familiar adults taken when they were children playing with toys or with toys in the shot – the older the better. Select groups of toys which represent a change over time, for example dolls in period costume to present-day dress, vehicles from veteran cars to present day motors, steam trains and modern trains.
- Show the photographs of previous generations playing with their toys and help the children to notice details about the toys.
- Show a toy group selection, say cars then and now, and discuss the changes in style and design, colour range, power and speed.
- Join in a game with the toys, if they are not too precious to be played with.

 Taking this further

Invite an older person to come in and talk to the children about the toys she/he played with and games she/he played when a child.

If anyone can loan toys of historical interest, involve the children in a hands-on investigation of their uses in the past.

Disability Awareness

EYFS aspect	Group size	Resources
Time Place Communities	1–4	Blacked-out, child-size goggles Headphones

This will help children gain a better understanding of disability.

- Begin by discussing with the children what they see and hear around them and ask them to try and imagine what it would be like if they could not see or hear.
- Ask for volunteers to experience what it is like to be deaf or partially deaf.
- Help the volunteers in turn to put on the headphones and try to listen to quiet voices from some distance across the room. Encourage them to say what it feels like.
- Discuss the ways the hearing-impaired can know what is said – using sign language, lip-reading, hearing aids.
- Move on to consider the blind or partially sighted and ask for volunteers to experience it.
- Help the volunteers in turn to negotiate part of the room while blindfold or wearing blacked-out goggles. Encourage them to say what it feels like and what clues they use to work out where they are and what is in front of them. Some, or all, may want to try with blurred goggles rather than completely black, and this will help the comparisons.
- Discuss the use of spectacles and the ways blind people 'see' – using Braille, guide dogs, white sticks, clues in what they hear and touch.
- Provide familiar objects for the children to feel with their eyes closed.
- Discuss other forms of physical disability, such as an inability to walk, and how they affect people's lives and are overcome.

Safety note
Remember that parts of this activity could be quite unnerving for some children, depending on their individual experiences.

Calling Planet Earth

EYFS aspect	Group size	Resources
Exploration and Investigation Designing and Making ICT Place	1–2	Access to a computer Giant cardboard box Any available 'astronaut' clothing

Take a journey into space and look back at Earth.

Preparation
Use a search engine to find websites and images of the Earth from space and save them in the computer ready for use in the game. If you have the software you could include them in a *PowerPoint* presentation which would make them easier to show, but it is not necessary if you have them easily accessible.

- Introduce the activity by talking about the sky, moon and stars and how it has been possible for astronauts to travel in spaceships and rockets.
- Build a space rocket with the children, using whatever junk materials you can find. Use a giant cardboard box for a capsule, large enough to take the children, but keep the space journey short. You can glue or tape yoghurt pot switches and pictures of dials to the inside.
- The children can dress in any clothing which looks like that of an astronaut, but imagination can serve just as well.
- Lift the children into the spaceship and carry out a controls check, for example 'Oxygen?' – 'Check', 'Door lock?' – 'Check'.
- Have the children help you count down and blast off.
- After travelling in space for a short while, land on the moon.
- The astronauts then take their place at the space centre control – the computer.
- Talk the children through the satellite views collected earlier, letting them change the images as much as possible.

Taking this further
This is an ideal theme for artwork.

It's a Sign

EYFS aspect	Group size	Resources
Place Communities	1–4	None

This is a communication game using face and hand signs.

With the children sitting in front of you, go through some visual signs with them:

- Finger to lips for quiet.
- Hand straight out in front for stop.
- Handshake.
- Cupped hand gesture for 'come here'.
- Crooked finger gesture for 'come here'.
- Indicating something by pointing to it.
- Hands together in 'prayer' for 'please'.
- Waving on with the hand.
- Waving hello/goodbye.
- Waving finger side-to-side for 'no'.
- Thumb/s-up for 'yes'.
- Nod/shake of the head for 'yes'/'no'.
- Happy face/delighted face.
- Sad face/crying face.
- Frown.
- Angry face.
- Frightened face.

Help the children to practise these signs.

Game 1: Give the children only hand and face directions without words:

- Shake hands with, bow or curtsey to each child with a smile.
- Count the children by pointing to each in turn, then count the same number on your fingers.
- Send each in turn to different parts of the room, giving adjustment signs with your finger/hand to make a precise position. Use frowns, smiles and, finally, thumbs-up when they are in the exact position.

- Beckon one child with a crooked finger or cupped hand.
- Indicate an object such as a plate of apple slices on a nearby table and gesture the child to pick it up and bring it to you.
- Offer the apple slices to the child.
- Use a sweeping hand gesture to get the child to offer the slices to others in the group.
- Use your arms to gesture everyone to come back together.

Game 2: The children respond to facial expression by putting their thumbs up for positive signs and thumbs down for negative signs:

- Leader smiles – children thumbs up.
- Leader frowns – children thumbs down.
- Leader nods – children thumbs up.
- Leader shakes head – children thumbs down.

Recycle It

EYFS aspect	Group size	Resources
Place Communities	1–4	Large collection of clean, empty food and drinks containers Plastic fruit and vegetables (or pictures of real fruit and vegetables) Scrap paper and an old newspaper Play money Shopping bags Toy shop till (optional)

Give a shopping game the recycling message.

- Set up a shopping game with lots of empty cartons, packets and plastic bottles, etc.
- Help the children to arrange the containers on reachable surfaces, rather like a shop.
- Help them to choose their shopping and pay at the till, placing everything in a shopping bag.
- When the shopping is brought 'home' sort it into various recycling categories, such as plastics, plastic bags, cans, paper, card and compostable (fruit and vegetable) material.
- Talk about where you take it next and where it goes from there, for example plastic bottles can become a plastic bucket.

Safety note
Do not use cans if they have sharp edges. Ensure that the carrier bags are child-safe.

IDEA

99

It Is My Belief

EYFS aspect	Group size	Resources
Exploration and Investigation ICT Place Communities	1–4	Digital camera Access to a computer

Take the children to visit a local place of worship.

You will need to contact the appropriate church, mosque or temple leader to arrange a visit. Go to the building beforehand to talk to those who will welcome the group, and familiarize yourself with what will be discovered and talked about. You will need to know about toilet facilities, especially if the visit is to last a long time. You will also need to obtain permissions from parents.

- Before entering the building, remind the children of the importance of respecting the beliefs and customs of others.
- Look at the outside of the building, photograph it and talk about it with the children.
- When inside the faith leader/s may well be happy to talk to the children.
- Help the children to focus on the internal structure and decoration of the building – look at the paintings and windows. Take photographs if permitted.
- Draw attention to the various sacred areas and special items essential to the act of worship represented, such as religious symbols and holy books.
- On return, let the children see you download the photographs onto a computer and then they can help you click through the images.
- Ask the children for their memories of the visit and remind them of the most important elements connected to the faith.

Safety note
Observe normal arrangements for taking children out and complete all regulatory forms.

Taking this further

Some places of worship will permit rubbings to be made. These are a simple and ideal memento of the visit.

Invite leaders of various faiths to visit the children and talk to them about how their followers worship.

Who Lives Here?

EYFS aspect	Group size	Resources
Designing and Making Place Communities	1–4	Large A4 envelopes Art materials Occupation-based pictures

Develop an understanding that people living nearby have different jobs.

Make a collection of occupation-based pictures (all the better if the appropriate person is shown in the picture), such as a window with a ladder and bucket for window cleaner; a spanner with car for mechanic; a soldier/police officer/nurse in uniform; hair dryer and scissors for hairdresser; plugs and wiring for electrician.

- With a marker pen, draw the outline of a large door on each of the envelopes (the pictures will go behind these doors eventually);
- Help the children to paint or colour the envelopes as house fronts, including windows and paying particular attention to the doors.
- When the houses are dry, cut the doors from one layer of the envelopes only and fold them back so they open easily. Stick a picture/picture set in each opening and close the doors to cover the pictures. Number the doors with a marker pen.
- Set the houses in a 'terrace' and ask the children to work out who lives in each one. There are a number of ways you can do this. First, ask the children in turn to choose a door and open it so that she/he (or everyone) can work it out. Alternatively, ask the children in turn to open a particular numbered door and work out the owner's occupation, or get them to open a particular coloured door and work out the job.
- When everyone has had a turn, the 'occupants' of the houses can move out and new residents (different pictures/picture sets) can move in for a continuation of the game.

Taking this further

Cut out a suitable size letterbox in the door so that a child can peep in and try to work out who lives there before the door is opened.